115

09

Palm
Reading

Palm Reading

discover the secrets hidden in your hand

hamlyn

Frank C. Clifford

This book is dedicated with love and appreciation
to my mother and to Roberto, Helen and Filly.
And to other members of my extended family for
their love and support: Nicola & Tim, George &
Marcel, Barbara & David, Rob, Kirstie & Ben, and
Marisa. And to Sally Fry who first taught me how
to read palms.

First published in Great Britain in 2004 by
Hamlyn, an imprint of Octopus Publishing Group Ltd
2–4 Heron Quays, London E14 4JP

Copyright © Octopus Publishing Group Ltd 2004

Distributed in the United States and Canada by
Sterling Publishing Co., Inc.
387 Park Avenue South, New York, NY 10016-8810

ISBN 0 600 60971 5

A CIP catalogue record for this book is available
from the British Library

Printed and bound in China

10 9 8 7 6 5 4 3 2 1

Contents

Introduction: the language of the hands

Your hands are living mirrors, reflecting your personality, needs and drives. They reveal your personal philosophies, and the talents you have inherited, as well as the ones that you are in the process of developing. Your hands show the important events and people from your past, and they give insights into the person you currently are today. They speak both of your self-perception as well as how you perceive the world around you.

Your hands are your personal autobiography, but not all the chapters have been written yet. By understanding the language of the hand, you can learn to communicate your needs, express your creative side and, indeed, influence your future. The choices you make and your reactions to the events and people you encounter all shape your life, and in turn, they shape the exisiting lines on your palms. The choices, actions and reactions of today will show in your hands tomorrow. You influence your environment and in turn, it also affects you. Your hands reflect this two-way process and are a living testament to the power you have to shape your destiny.

For many people, their biggest handicap is an unwillingness to learn from life and a refusal to take responsibility for their own life paths.

Palm-reading is one tool for those who seek self-understanding so that they may be more self-determining. It is not something that is recommended for those who want to be told of an unalterable future. While it can often 'foretell' upcoming events, the secret to palmistry is that knowledge of the hands gives you control over your life and future. The future is negotiable.

Learning to read palms opens up a whole world of insight, but it is a lot easier than many people think. When interpreting the palm, there is room for many commonsense associations, and these will help you to remember meanings quickly and more easily. Here are two examples.

• Reddish, warm, broad and well-padded palms show a warmth of spirit and a healthy appetite for living. Pale, cold and narrow hands reveal an emotional reserve.

• The head line governs the way that you process ideas. The line can either be straight or curved. When you hear the word 'straight' you may think of words such as direct, balanced, consistent, conformist, orderly, unbending. Indeed a straight head line reveals a practical mentality. This person works from A to B in a straightforward manner. The word 'curved' brings up notions of bending, flexibility, meandering, taking a new turn. A curved head line suggests a mentality that is more lateral in its thinking. Such a person would think of new ways of working or approaching a problem.

This book is designed to offer quick readings on the most important lines in the hand. Being a 'cookbook' of interpretations, you must bear in mind that a few profiles may contradict each other. This may be a reflection of your own inner contradictions but the art of palmistry lies in synthesizing these various aspects to allow and enable you to become more of the person you are meant to be.

How to use this book

The book is divided into five easy-to-follow sections.

In Part One, **Getting Started**, you will learn to recognize both hand size and the four categories of hand shape. An understanding of these will reveal your basic approach and character motivations. Then you will note the fundamental differences between the left and right hands, and look at how the overall quantity of palm lines reveals the complexity of your responses.

Part Two, **The Major Palm Lines**, examines the four main palm lines – the life line, the head line, the heart line and the fate line – in detail, as well as their courses and various line markings found on the hand.

Part Three, **Minor Lines and Special Markings**, examines all the other lines and marks found on your palm.

In Part Four, **Hand Topography**, you will learn about the various areas of the hand, including the fingers, the fingerprint patterns and the fleshy mounts on the palm.

In Part Five, **Timing the Hand**, you will learn how to 'time' the hand, or work out when certain significant events took place.

Instant readings

In the main sections of the book, there are numerous self-contained profiles of line formations or markings. Each self-contained profile is accompanied by an illustration and given a threefold interpretation relating to:

Personality
character insights
and motivations

Love
romantic expectations
and relationship needs

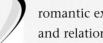

Work
professional attitudes,
aptitudes, money and
ambition

1

Getting Started

The lines on your palms are undoubtedly the most interesting parts of your hand and provide many answers to your most important questions. By first understanding the overall impression of the hands, however, you can gain important insights into your personality, basic needs, drives and motivations. The shape, texture and size of your hands, as well as the amount of lines on your palm, all contribute vital information about your temperament, and provide a solid foundation for understanding the language of the hands.

Left and right hands

One of the most common questions a palmist hears is 'Which hand do you read?' Most palmists look at both hands to provide a more complete picture of their client's temperament. Yet there is some debate as to the different areas of life assigned to each hand. Traditional palmists believe the two hands show different facets of one's personality, that the markings shown on the left hand show your potential while the markings on the right will reveal how much of this potential you tap into (left = what you are born with; right = what you make of yourself).

Many modern palmists don't believe it is as simple as this – potential is everywhere in the hand and lines change on both hands. Each hand reveals a particular type of potential as well as past reactions, present circumstances and future possibilities – but the left shows your personal responses to all these matters, while the right shows how you respond to, and interact with, the world outside your personal environment on a professional or social level. Events that register on the left hand are those that have a profound personal effect on what is often your most private self. Events that are seen as markings on the right hand, however, are those (personal or otherwise) that affect your public life and the way you function in the outside world.

The two hands

The left hand – regardless of whether you are right- or left-handed – will always reveal more about your real self. It is the hand that reveals your psychological dynamics and motivations – particularly those formed by early experiences. It shows the events that you internalize and the deeper issues and emotions that you ponder, analyse and reflect upon. Usually only those closest to you whom you trust – family, partners, soul mates – will get to encounter the person you really are – your insecurities, private dreams, childhood issues – and this person is revealed in your left hand.

The right hand is who you are in public and when 'on show', consciously wishing to project an image. Markings on this hand will show the abilities that you manifest in your working life and how you can achieve success financially and professionally. The right hand can show fame, success and riches – the sort that can be measured in public terms – but the left hand shows the extent of your personal sense of fulfilment and spiritual purpose.

The left hand is linked to music, imagination, creativity, emotion, memory and intuition. The right hand is associated with language, business sense, calculation, science and reasoning.

HAND RULERSHIPS

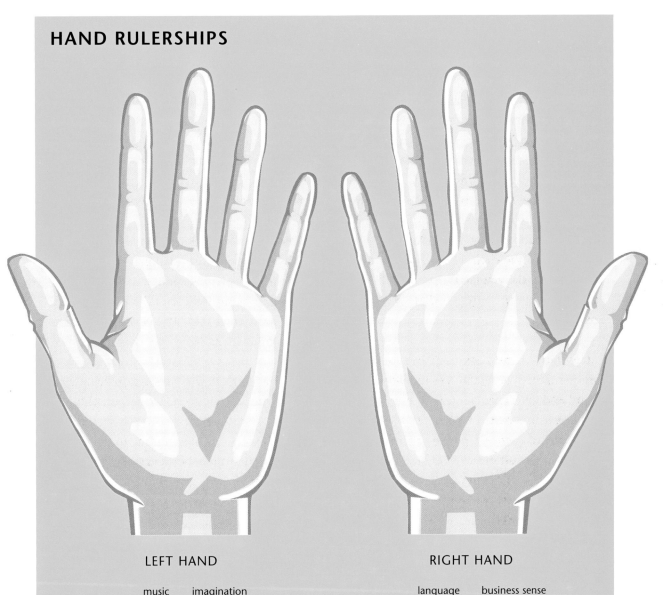

LEFT HAND

music   imagination
creativity emotion
memory   intuition

RIGHT BRAIN

RIGHT HAND

language   business sense
calculation science
reasoning   materialism

LEFT BRAIN

Full and empty palms

Some hands are covered with a network of lines, looking like a spider's web of intricate criss-cross patterns. Others have three or four major lines and very little else. Lines are not formed by manual work (although certain exercises and activities may add greater emphasis to particular lines). It is interesting to note that builders and other manual workers often have fewer lines than those who rarely use their hands in their work. Science has shown that the major lines (and fingerprints) are already formed on the hands of unborn babies by the fifth month of pregnancy.

At a glance

When you study hands, you will notice that there are often wide differences across race and gender. It is important to remember that women often have 'busier' palms than men, so be careful before jumping to conclusions. In addition, the left hand often has more lines on it than the right. Some races have fewer lines on their palms than others, so keep these basic differences in mind and only make the following assessments if the palms differ widely from what is expected.

A quick look at whether your palms are full or empty can say much about the weight of emotional burdens you carry, as well as your level of neurosis. More lines on the hand suggest you respond greatly to people and situations in your life; you

FULL PALM

If you have palms full of many fine lines, you are hyper-sensitive and should avoid negative people who drain you.

therefore tend to take on board more information as well as the feelings and anxieties of those around you. With fewer lines, you don't pick up atmospheres or other people's concerns so readily. You stay on track attending to your own needs as well as the needs of those in – and beyond – your immediate circle.

Full palms

Highly sensitive, impressionable, vulnerable, intuitive, receptive and responsive. A sponge that is able to absorb information and pick up discord. Easily moved to an emotional response. Expressive. An emotional barometer, prone to worry, anxiety and neurosis. The drama queen. Highly strung and often very nervous, with the possibility of depression and anxiety-related ailments, yet eventually displaying great emotional resilience and able to carry heavy emotional burdens and endure more stressful situations than most.

EMPTY PALM

With only the major lines present, you are more self-protective but should express your needs to avoid a build-up of stress.

Empty palms

Appears less emotionally complex. Would prefer to block out or sidestep deep emotional situations. Often labelled insensitive to others. Steady, inflexible, not easily swayed, a black-or-white approach, with an impenetrable front. Enjoys creature comforts and the good, simple life. Physically resilient and vigorous, but exerts energy in short, sharp bursts.

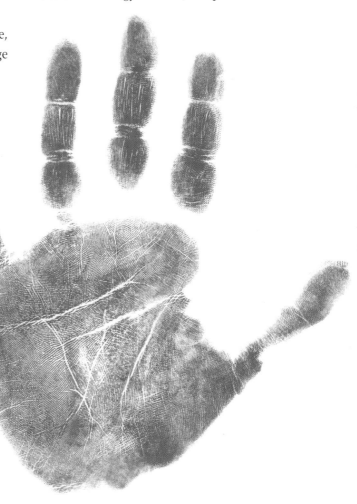

Assessing the whole hand

Size

You can check the size of your hands by judging them in relation to the rest of your body. One way of working this out is to compare your hands to the length of your face. An average hand should extend from the chin to the middle of the forehead.

The proportional size of your hands tells much about how you tackle tasks and projects, whether you are suited to focusing on detail or managing large endeavours. Your head line (see page 36) will say much about your talents, but the size of your hands gives an insight into your basic method of operation.

Large hands Somewhat surprisingly, and contrary to general expectation, with large hands you have greater ability to focus on detailed work than those with small hands. Someone who plays a musical instrument, paints or crafts small objects (or anything intricate) will invariably have large hands. In general, with large hands your actions are slower than those around you, as you take your time to do things 'just right'. There is a very strong note of perfectionism here (particularly if the fingers or head line are long; see pages 110 and 42), and you are prepared to put in the necessary hours to perfect your craft. You excel in situations in

FLEXIBILITY

Palmistry is full of simple, commonsense associations.
Here are some relating to how flexible your hands and fingers are.

Firm hands	Resolute and purposeful temperament.
Stiff hands	Inability to be swayed, stubbornness.
Supple hands	Flexibility.
Very supple hands	Malleable, easily dominated by stronger characters.
Flexible fingertips	Adaptable, 'easy come, easy go' attitude.
Rigid fingertips	Inflexible attitude.

which careful planning and detailed work are prerequisites. Sometimes you start to lose track of the larger, overall picture because you are so fixated on fine-tuning matters. You are attracted to detailed work that takes advantage of your strong powers of concentration and ability to take pains. You should allow others to take control of the overall running of a business while you concentrate on attending to the small print. In relationships, you make thoughtful, attentive partners who remember that it is often the smallest things that make up a great romance.

Small hands Why doesn't everyone work as fast as you do? Why do others waste their time procrastinating and attending to insignificant details? With small hands, you cut to the chase, want everything done yesterday and pride yourself on your ability to think and act faster than those around you. In love, you need someone who can match your speed and live in the fast lane, and can be irritable and impatient with slower folk. At work, you thrive when faced with challenge and a packed diary, and you love to instigate new projects, juggle half a dozen ideas as well as act in managerial or supervisory roles. You don't want to spend time wrapped up in red tape or analysing data, you want to take action based on preliminary tests and half-finished plans.

You look for situations that make good use of your initiative and ambition, so jobs with opportunities to get ahead suit you best. You have an ability to see the larger picture as well as the finishing line. With small hands, you are the proverbial hare racing past the tortoise to the finishing line but, unless you ensure all matters have been attended to, you may find that you have been overtaken by your slower counterpart.

Skin texture

As you might expect, coarse skin is found on those of you who may not be the most sensitive or diplomatic. You are, however, able to cope with most things that life throws your way, and you have an ability to 'rough it' when necessary. Perseverance and determination, possibly as a result of a tough upbringing, are key traits. There may also be impatience with others who cannot cope as well as you do.

In adulthood, when the skin is soft it shows an appreciation of the finer things, as well as an artistic bent. When very soft, you may be a little too fond of the good life and willing to let others do everything for you. When the hand is soft and flabby, it can be a sign of over-indulgence, laziness or comfort eating.

When assessing the skin texture, it is important to consider the person's age and the work they do.

Hand shape

Your hand's shape will reveal your basic motivations as well as the fundamental way in which you experience life. Many modern palmists use the fourfold division based upon the four elements: fire, earth, air and water. In the next section you will be learning to assess and interpret these four hand shapes.

It is important to become acquainted with the basic hand shapes. An understanding of these begins with simple interpretations of palm shape and finger length.

Palm shape

The palm shape is assessed by measuring the palm from the wrist to the base of the middle finger and comparing it to the width of the palm (from the outside of the palm to the fleshy mound lying beside the thumb). With *square* palms (earth and air hands), where the measurements are very similar, you are keen to be practical and productive. With *rectangular* palms (water and fire hands), where one measurement is longer than the other, you rely on intuitive hunches and are driven by emotion.

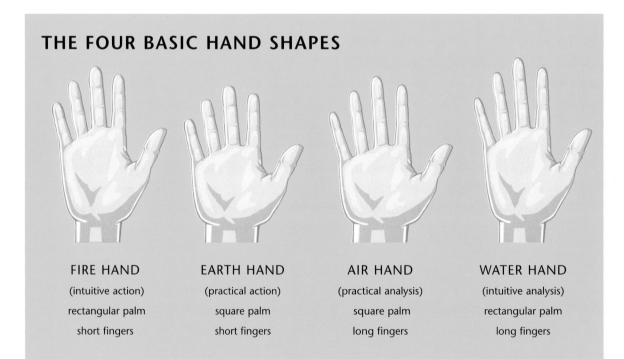

THE FOUR BASIC HAND SHAPES

FIRE HAND	EARTH HAND	AIR HAND	WATER HAND
(intuitive action)	(practical action)	(practical analysis)	(intuitive analysis)
rectangular palm	square palm	square palm	rectangular palm
short fingers	short fingers	long fingers	long fingers

Finger length

The finger length is best determined by measuring the fingers from the back of the hand (from knuckle to the nail tip) and seeing how this measures up to the length of the palm (from the wrist to the base of the middle finger). Fingers are considered long when they are of equal or greater length to the palm. With *long* fingers (found on air and water hands), you take time to process information, analyse and plan strategies. *Short* fingers (found on earth and fire hands) are a sign that you are able to grasp and assimilate all the essential components quickly, avoid analysis and are action-orientated – you just get on with it. (There is more information about finger length on page 110.)

Other variations

Many people have hands that don't naturally fit into one hand shape. For example, some have an earth-type hand but may have an array of sensitive lines more akin to the water type. If this is the case, it is important to stick to the simple classifications above and not to put too much emphasis on hand shape when analysing character in depth. The fingerprint patterns, as well as the individual finger length and the course of all the major lines will help to bring both depth and detail to any analysis.

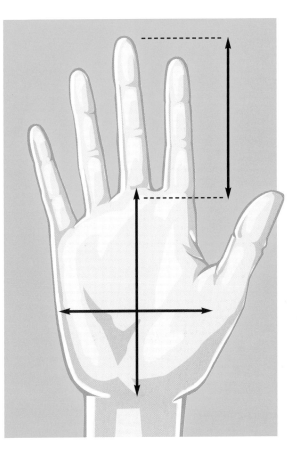

PALM SHAPE

This diagram shows you how to determine whether your palm is square or rectangular, and how to assess your finger length.

Occasionally, the left hand is of a different shape to that of the right hand. This fascinating disparity suggests a somewhat contradictory, 'split' character, and one that often displays very different personal and professional lives.

Fire hand

A rectangular palm with short fingers; many deep lines; whorl or tented arch fingerprints; energy and direction in the lines.

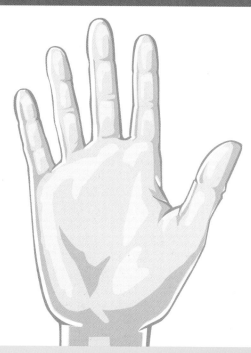

Work

For you, work needs to be a calling. You need enlightening work that you feel passionate about. Often money is a means to an end, and you prefer glory and acclaim over financial security any time. You thrive in a job that gives you a spotlight and puts you centre stage. You can inspire others but should avoid careers such as politics and the law in which diplomacy and patience are prerequisites. You would sleepwalk through your working life if you found yourself trapped in an office sifting through endless paperwork. You are at your best promoting yourself or the talents of others, but be careful of impetuous moves that leave you with little security.

Love

Your need for excitement is most apparent in relationships. You seek partners who are pioneers prepared to push back the boundaries and those who exhibit an adventurous streak. For you, sex is a natural and necessary way of expressing all your feelings, although partners of other hand shapes may want to explore feelings or resolve conflicts before jumping into action. Your need for variety can lead to a seven-year itch (or even a seven-month itch) as you bore easily and crave new challenges. You abhor settling down into a fixed routine – predictability will sound the death knell of any relationship.

Personality

You are driven to experience excitement and adventure. You seek challenge but life is frustrating when there are no dragons to slay or causes to fight. Faith is an important theme in your life, as it motivates you to live life to the fullest, to gamble on hunches and make big leaps that require courage and risk. Energy and enthusiasm are traits that you have in abundance and these are also traits that you inspire in others.

Earth hand

A square palm with short fingers; empty palms but broad and deep major lines; often arch or loop fingerprints.

Personality

You know that in order to succeed you must apply yourself systematically, work hard and plan ahead. You are intent on constructing a firm foundation for your future. Taking risks is usually for others. You hate to waste time, money or energy. You look for value, expediency and profitability in all you encounter. Creature comforts are important and you are motivated by financial reward, which gives you the security you crave. It is important that you find ways of expressing yourself physically without neglecting your emotions. You strive for routine and feel secure in a world that is predictable and manageable.

Work

Where is the proof? Never one to believe something without seeing it for yourself and putting it to the test, you need to learn from hands-on application and need to experience life first-hand. You need to work practically and slowly to absorb new ideas. Being paid well is a necessity, as it is a statement of your achievement and status in the outside world. Work that gets you back in touch with the physical realm, such as building and gardening, will be therapeutic and give you the results you need from your labours. Try to avoid a build-up of stress, learn to unwind after work and express yourself through sports or physical activity.

Love

You aim to be a dependable partner who can offer others security and comfort. Expressing your emotional needs may be tough, though, and you often feel lonely or misunderstood. You need to get in touch with your sensuality and learn to articulate your physical and emotional needs. Partners should understand that you are motivated by financial security and you need to establish foundations before you can venture forth, make a move or take risks. But sometimes it takes forever for you to move forward.

Air hand

A square palm with long fingers; long, strong clear lines; a variety of fingerprints but many loops; a triangular shape to the palm and often a curve on the percussion side.

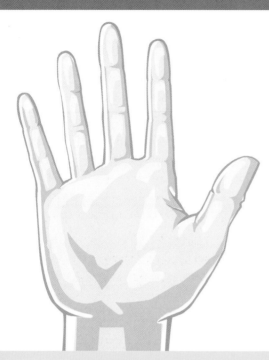

Work

Your work needs to be stimulating and teach you things you never knew. Work in the communication fields is ideal, and whether you write, teach, sell or work with computers, you will need a telephone and diary close by. Even if you work by yourself, you still need to interact with others, bouncing off ideas and sharing stories. It is likely that you will do a number of jobs (often at the same time) but your challenge is to produce concrete results and stay in one position long enough to make your mark.

Love

Partners soon discover that, although you have bags of charm and quick wit, you sometimes need to disengage from them. At times you have a desire to detach from others and avoid heavy emotional scenes. Ideas, observations and discussions are more interesting to you than emotional dramas, so you need a partner who fires up your mind and is not afraid of having a healthy argument to clear the air. Intimate partners will eventually demand that you share more than just your ideas with them. You may be forced to probe your deeper emotions, which you usually keep safely locked away.

Personality

You are a 'Peter Pan' personality, full of youthful enthusiasm and curiosity. You seek to understand life and are motivated by finding answers to all the many questions you have. New ideas and options are constantly on the horizon, but which one will you choose? Trying to juggle them all will lead to very little being accomplished. Setting clear, realistic goals but keeping a variety of avenues open is ideal for you. Putting pressure on yourself to be all things to all people will cause nervous tension and irritability. Alert, expressive and versatile, you live in your head, but you must remember to feed your body too.

Water hand

A rectangular palm with long fingers; many feathery and deep lines; often pointed fingertips; loop fingerprints that reach high on to the tip.

Personality

You feel things more deeply than most and are able to tap into your emotions as well as the emotional states of others around you. You have a strong curiosity and need to understand hidden motivations, raw emotions and life's mysteries. Others see you as a sensitive, impressionable, nurturing and caring friend. Your biggest challenge is to fight your own self-doubt and pessimism and start believing in yourself. Avoid creating emotional crises in order to be understood and supported. Ask others for practical help rather than seeking a response via emotional blackmail.

Work

Work is satisfying only when you are receiving an emotional response from others. You need to serve, advise and support, so employment in the caring professions would be ideal. All types of healing appeal to you, whether it is healing the emotional scars of clients as a counsellor or building a bridge of understanding between opposing factions. Fashion and artistic work also attract your eye. Whatever your job, you bring sensitivity, empathy and understanding to your position – but ensure that your own personal dramas do not start to interfere with your professional life.

Love

You must safeguard yourself against negative, needy people who pull you down and chip away at your self-confidence. Sometimes it is easy to lose yourself in relationships, to take the form your partner wishes rather than standing firm and refusing to be influenced. But who's really controlling whom? You have a strong need to make emotional contact with a partner in order to belong, and this makes you malleable as well as manipulative. Yet sooner or later you realize that, in order for relationships to be fulfilling, you must share yourself without giving up your identity or trying to force others to change by using passive aggression or subtle scheming.

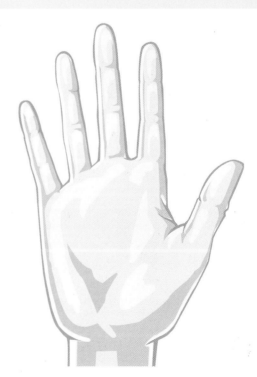

The Major Palm Lines

After studying the general shape of the hands, the next step is to begin understanding the major lines that sweep across the landscape of the palms. Lines represent your energy drives. For example, the life line is your physical energy, the head line reveals your type of mental and intellectual energy, the heart line says much about your emotional energy, and the fate line reveals the amount of energy you have to direct into work, responsibilities and ambitions.

Energy flow

Picture each palm line as symbolizing a river. Studying its course, colour and depth will reveal both the strength and direction of the river's flow. A palm line that is broad and clear shows the river is strong and direct – indicating that you have a strong sense of purpose in that area. When a line is weak or feathery, the river's strength is less powerful and could easily dissipate – it warns of being half-hearted or negative in your approach; it is important to 'toughen up' *in the area represented by the line* (for example, the head line shows how you apply your mind and cope with stress). In addition, an interrupted (broken) palm line indicates hesitancy or that a situation has forced you to stop and question the path on which you are travelling. An uninterrupted line suggests that the 'energy' represented is free-flowing and can operate without interruption.

Thickness of the lines

When lines are very thick, it shows that you are pushing yourself too far, perhaps working too hard or expecting too much from yourself. When palm lines are faint, however, it is as though you don't have the energy to provide a healthy balance in your life.

Duality

Palm lines have a twofold application. They both reveal character traits that you have developed and, if you use the timing charts at the back of this book, they can also show events that played a part in triggering these personality traits.

The dominant line

As with your hand shape (see pages 16–21), the four lines can be categorized by element. Some palmists use different classifications, but astrologers have commented on the link between each line and a particular element. Sometimes one line is stronger than the rest. Perhaps one is more complex than the others. Some people may have a Simian line, which will dominate the palm landscape.

If one particular line stands out, it is likely that its general meaning (and specific meaning from its shape and course) dominates your life. Sometimes all but one of the major lines appear to be of equal importance. The weakest line is in some ways your 'Achilles' heel', so take more notice of the profiles written about this line that are specific to your hand. On occasion, the standout line (whether the strongest or weakest link) will differ from the left to the right hands, and the difference in meaning here should also be considered.

If one line is missing or weak, you have difficulty expressing that element. If one line dominates the hand, then that line or element is the one that dominates your life.

THE FOUR MAJOR PALM LINES

Dominant line	Element	Relevant qualities
Life line	Fire	Enthusiasm, energy, challenge, physicality
Head line	Air	Ideas, reasoning, questioning, communication, exchange
Heart line	Water	Emotions, impressions, moods, perception
Fate line	Earth	Practicalities, money, security, stability, routine

The arrows show the direction in which most palmists read and time them.

note: The Simian line (see page 68) is a combination of air and water.

In the following sections, you will learn that where each of the major lines begin and where they terminate will have a great deal to say about your approach, personality and future. The depth, course, relative position and general appearance of the lines, plus any markings found, will all say much about your life and character. Each major line will describe your approach to work, love and life, as well as reveal many of the events that take place.

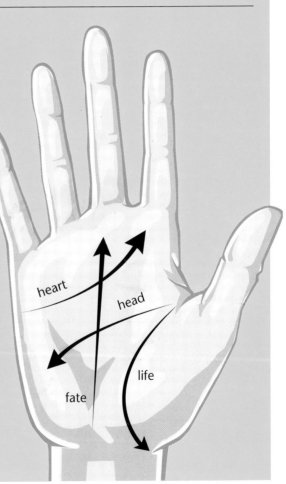

Life line

How much energy, vigour and physical stamina do you have? Do you actively engage in life and pursue opportunities, travel and challenges? Or has your 'get up and go' gone off and left? When the going gets tough, do you throw in the towel or come out fighting? Studying your life line will tell all.

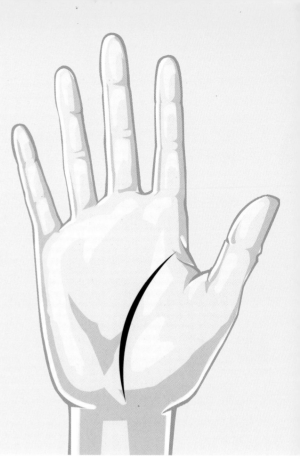

Understanding the course, strength and markings on the life line will reveal how much you get involved in life and whether you have direction and purpose. Are you one of life's bystanders or a major player in the driving seat chasing your dreams? Will difficulties send you off course, or inspire you to travel into uncharted waters? The life line will reveal the extent of your self-determination and enthusiasm for life. It also says much about your ability to tackle obstacles, move ahead with confidence and live life to the full. It shows the levels of your spirit, zest, virility and drive. It provides strong clues as to your physical strength and health, as well as your ability to bounce back from illness. The left hand's life line will reveal inherited health predispositions, inner reserves of courage and your enthusiasm to strive for a fulfilling personal life, while the right shows the extent of your stamina and drive in the outside world.

Shape and form

This line usually begins at the inside edge of the hand. Some life lines are longer, broader or clearer than others. The line is read from the top towards the wrist, as it wraps around the ball of the thumb. Some palmists also read it from the bottom up (in conjunction with the fate line) and research into this has thrown up some very interesting findings.

Often events in the individual's early life – from childhood to their mid-20s – will be shown here.

Missing

It is rare for the life line to be missing. Often it is short (see page 30), but this does not indicate a short lifespan. The life line is the quality of your life, not your longevity. Short or missing, it suggests that you need to be more passionate and involved in life. When missing in part (and often backed up by a Mars line – see page 89) you must weather the storm of change or ill health before you feel ready to take on the world again.

Remember that the life line can fade out or strengthen over time as well as develop additional strands, islands or branches. These developments 'coincide' with the changes you make to your inner (left hand) and outer (right hand) lives. For example, changing your diet or exercise routine will see a corresponding change in your hands.

Starting point

The life line usually begins halfway between the index finger and thumb, but when it begins higher up (from the direction of the index finger), this is a sign of early confidence in youth – and you think you are naturally entitled to the best of everything. When it enters from the mount of lower Mars (see page 109), there is the potential to accomplish much, but you should take care not to alienate others with your combative, pugnacious streak.

Duality

The life line can be read on two levels. It discloses your *psychological attitudes* to your life's journey (issues of health, travel, family and romance), as well as the *actual events* you experience in these areas. (You will learn to time the latter on page 121.)

Markings on the life line

Any marking, formation or crossing bar on this line will reveal physical and psychological changes to your immediate environment, family, health and fitness. See the individual sections that follow for specific markings, as well as the feature on pages 90–1.

Relating

A fine line that runs parallel to (and a millimetre inside) the life line will show an important person (such as a parent, partner or mentor) in your life who moulds or inspires you. This person is travelling by your side supporting and guiding you. Time the life line (using the chart on page 121) to see the ages during which this effect will be most felt.

Children's hands

Don't be dismayed if your child has a short life line or one that has a series of small island-like formations, giving the line a 'chained' appearance. This is a common feature, reflecting the usual health concerns and adjustments all children encounter. The line can, and often does, strengthen and develop in the teenage years.

Strong, dominant life line

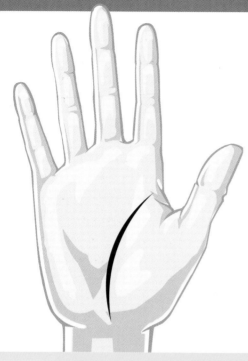

Work

Your life line won't reveal the kind of work you do, but a very strong line will indicate that you need work that enables you to compete, get ahead and move up the ladder. Others would benefit if you took on the role of group leader and motivator, but you prefer to focus on your own projects and lead by example. It is hardly surprising that a life line that shows robust health and a strong constitution could be utilized to great effect in sports, outdoor pursuits, gardening and any type of martial art or weight training. Work that requires strong physical endurance, resilience and dedication fits the bill.

Love

Potential partners should beware: in pursuit of the full life you demand much time expressing yourself under the sheets. Sex is a basic and necessary outlet for all your free-flowing physical energy but remember to make the experience satisfying for all parties concerned. You know better than most that a varied, fulfilling sex life will keep you youthful and that it keeps the fires burning at home. Partners will always be left in no doubt as to whether you are still interested in them. When the base of your palm is wide, this suggests stamina and virility, making you an athlete in and out of the bedroom.

Personality

You understand instinctively that to succeed in any area of life you need the three Ds: discipline, determination and drive. Your aim is to venture forth in all areas with confidence and you are determined to tackle life head on. You know that the secret of life is in the living – and you want to be living life to the full. When the thumb is strong too, you give off an indomitable air of self-assurance, power and vitality. Others sense that with you around, tasks will be completed and things will be done thoroughly. They also know that you have little time for those who do not want to take chances or who moan about their predicament.

Fine, feathery or faint life line

Personality

A general theme in life with this type of life line is a hesitancy to push yourself out into the world. More often than not, it is a psychological block rather than a physical impediment or condition. Sometimes it is a lack of confidence and an inhibiting shyness or timidity; at other times it is indecision or a 'who cares anyway?' attitude. It is important not to sideline yourself or play the victim. Rather than constantly reacting to events, it is vital that you develop a stronger appetite for life, get out there and make things happen. The key to living a fuller life lies in self-understanding and giving yourself permission to make mistakes.

Work

Finding work that you can be passionate and enthusiastic about is essential. Take more calculated risks and have the courage to journey into the professional unknown. Don't look too far into the future, however. Instead pour your energies into making a current project or course as fulfilling as possible, and move on when it ceases to be fruitful. Otherwise you will always be wondering if the grass is greener somewhere else. You may often avoid being in the driver's seat professionally, but you could benefit from taking on a leadership role – it will strengthen your self-belief, focus and determination.

Love

Sexually, a weak life line does not mean you won't have a fulfilling sex life, but it does suggest that other matters – anxieties, negative emotions, feeling victimized – get in the way and numb your sexual impulses. General depression or frustration with your life can do much to subdue your enthusiasm for lovemaking. The most important point to remember is not to become lethargic or apathetic with your partner and in your sex life. Sometimes, though, with this marking you place sex too highly on your agenda, thinking that it compensates for feelings of inadequacy or insecurity.

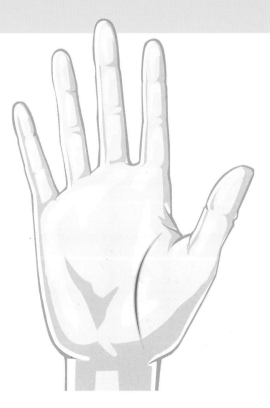

Short life line

Love

With this marking comes a childlike view of expecting every problem in relationships to be resolved quickly. Developing a long-term view of relationships, without feeling the pressure to make major commitments, will help to put all matters in perspective. Cultivate family relations and friendships with like-minded people, even if there are many around you who are prepared to cut their losses and move on.

Work

Your work often requires discipline and daily grind, but you have a strong resistance to this. Avoid jobs where you are swamped by emotions or forced to deal with competition and deadlines, as you don't particularly want much responsibility on your shoulders. Short-term and project work is favoured. There may come a time in your working life when you want to slow down or stop altogether and move into a lifestyle that is less stressful. With a short life line, anywhere away from the pressures of the rat race would suit you, preferably with a warm climate and relaxed attitudes.

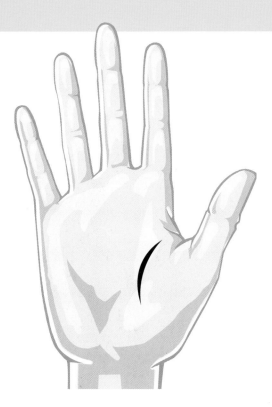

Personality

Staying power may not be your strong point, but dedication, tenacity and focus are invaluable traits to develop. It is vital that you don't take the easy option or throw in the towel when the going gets tough. There may be a side to you that believes in the negative adage 'all good things must come to an end', rather than believing in your own ability to run your life. When on the left hand only, this is a sign that you feel detached from your family or ancestors. Perhaps your family moved around so often there was a feeling of rootlessness in childhood, or maybe situations at home seemed as though they could change irrevocably at any point, leaving you feeling insecure about the future.

Overlapping life lines

Sometimes two life lines appear on the hand, and often there is a distinct overlap between the old and new life lines. This signifies a period of adjustment to the new lifestyle and outlook as old ties are slowly severed or the process of letting go takes its time. The higher up on the hand, the sooner the transition occurs. With overlaps, look out for a square over the lines. This often suggests that a routine or the support of a loved one may help this transition. The overlap between the life lines (a) and (b) can be timed using the life line timing chart on page 121.

Formation a

With this formation, an event or relationship causes you to venture forth on your own. You become more involved in the world at large and new interaction forces you to re-evaluate the past and the person you are. This marking means that you could probably divide your life into two chapters: before and after self-discovery. It shows a definite change in attitude and outlook, where you take control of your life and are intent on pursuing your own dreams. Sometimes it is with the help of faith or therapy; at other times it is a basic need for survival that forces you to emerge from your shell. Freedom and independence accompany this liberating, self-focused period.

Formation b

There is a side to you that needs to withdraw from the treadmill of work duties or daily grind. Perhaps difficulties have taken you away from your original plans. Your reaction is to retreat to find solitude and peace of mind, but you must not give up your dreams entirely. A change of focus is what is called for, rather than throwing in the towel. Sometimes with this marking there is a shift towards the helping professions, and you may consider turning your talents towards one-to-one work.

This overlap is more likely to occur near the wrist, when there is a natural inclination to slow down. At this point, doctors may advise you to give up your hectic lifestyle, but it is vital not to become scared by life or over-protective of your health. Keep your sense of adventure, take it easy but never consider retirement – always have a vocation or hobby.

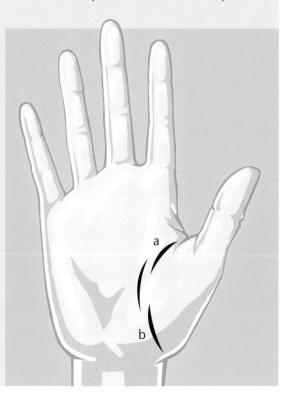

Two life lines of equal strength

Personality

Even if the burdens from relationships or work sometimes get you down, you still have a firmness and clarity of purpose that enables you to keep moving ahead. Your physical strength, resilience and never-say-die temperament see you win most of the confrontations in your life, and your forcefulness and fighting spirit ensure that you encounter more than most. You view life as hard work, but it is an uphill struggle that you are determined to win. Whatever your physical frame, there is a strength in your constitution that sees you fight off illness, fatigue and stress.

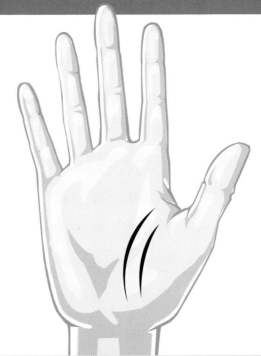

Work

Two jobs, a handful of dependants, numerous responsibilities? No problem! You expect life to be a fight for financial survival and you are always ready to enter the fray. Your head line will show the type of work to which you are best suited, but with a double life line you should consider work that utilizes your physical strength and stamina.

Love

Friends won't be shocked to learn that you often carry more than your fair share of the physical and emotional burdens of a relationship. You may spend time looking after loved ones who do not have your strong recuperative powers. Partners respect your fighting spirit, but may object when your pugnacious manner enters the emotional arena. They will certainly experience your intensity first-hand, as well as a terse response when things don't go according to plan. What most people don't realize is that, because you took on responsibilities from an early age, you have an underdeveloped emotional side and often experience rather a lack of confidence in personal relationships.

Short life line taken over by another line

A short life line substituted by another line does not signify a short life. As in the examples below, the life line is often replaced by another line (usually another life line, the fate line or a Mars line). See the life line timing chart on page 121 to pinpoint the year in which the life line ends.

The fate line takes over

When the fate line takes over from the life line, your routine or security may end at this stage and you need to begin again. It is an opportunity for a new start, but as this shift often occurs in later years change is more challenging. Energy and stamina may be lacking (no life line) but duty calls and there are bills to be paid (the fate line takes over).

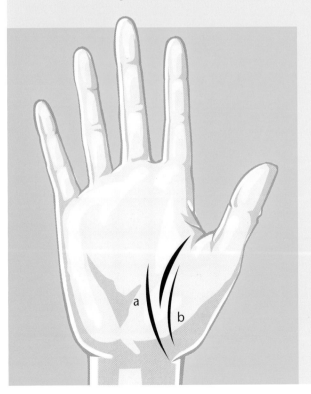

Sometimes it suggest you are on automatic pilot personally (left hand) or professionally (right hand). It may, however, be a time when you must summon up all your reserves of energy to start afresh.

Another life line takes over

An alternative to this position is when the life line is substituted by another life line originating from the wrist (a). This is a sign of needing to turn one's life around. Perhaps this is changing your working or living environments, or it may be linked to a health decision. Palmist Malcolm Wright has seen this feature on the hands of recovering alcoholics who have needed to turn their lives around. On the left hand, it suggests alcoholism may be in the family background.

The Mars line takes over

If the Mars line (see page 89) takes over from where the life line left off (b), it is a sign of sheer willpower, pugnacity and strength of character. This means that, whatever your physical condition in later life, you recognize that the will to live is stronger than your body's ailments.

Branches rising from life line

If you think of the life line as symbolizing a tree (with its roots near the wrist), then these rising lines could be seen as branches looking to grow and develop into new areas. To qualify, these branches must rise from the life line rather than cut through it (see pages 90–1).

Towards the index finger

These branches are often known as 'ambition lines', as they reveal a need to push yourself forward. The key here is that you are looking to improve your current circumstances. When rising in the early part of the life line (from the teenage years), it can show academic prizes. Usually, however, it shows that you feel restricted and need to break away from the confines of family or schooling.

When a long, prominent line rises towards the index finger, it is a definite sign of an effort to break away from an area in which you feel controlled or isolated. It may be the time you leave home or split from a partner. This mark of independence reveals a concerted effort to fend for yourself. Many fine rising lines point to a restless person who looks to achievements as a way of winning attention. When rising later in the hand, this is a sure sign of beginning a self-directed role in a personal (left hand) or professional (right hand) sphere.

Towards the middle finger

These branches indicate times when you take on greater responsibilities. It may be that you invest more time and effort in your work or must raise money for a new project – either personal or professional. Either way, it is a burden that feels like a coming of age.

Towards the ring finger

A rare branch, it indicates a happy and creative time. It suggests that ambitions are fulfilled after great effort and discipline. For a performer or artist, it will be a time of acclaim and recognition.

Towards the little finger

These are short rising lines, not health lines (page 91) or other lines cutting the life line (page 90). With this line there is an increase in funds following an investment or business venture.

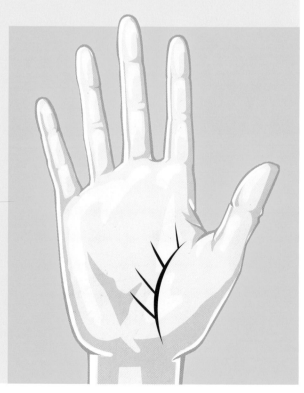

Other features on life line

Island at start of the line

Traditionally a sign of a mystery birth (i.e. illegitimacy), it also can denote that you suffered ill health as a child or that you felt isolated, lonely or misunderstood by your family and/or your peers.

Early break

A sign of shyness or sensitivity, this indicates that you made an effort to reinvent your life and strengthen your resolve.

Dot on the life line

A dot looks like a small crater made by pushing a pencil into the skin. This can indicate a temporary health concern often caused by stress.

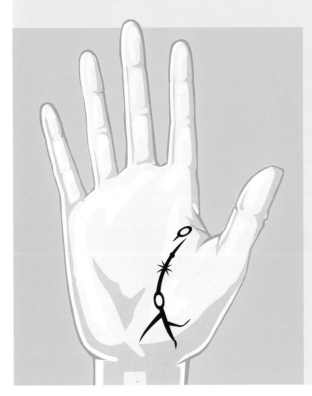

Star on the life line

Sometimes this indicates a profound shock to the system caused by an unexpected change in health and/or environment.

Island formation near the end of the line

At this time, you may feel isolated or hemmed in. This feeling of restriction could coincide with ill health, a relationship change or the realization that you are in the wrong job. You have a strong desire to find a way out of your current predicament, and need some objective advice.

Short fork off the life line

Considered a lucky sign, guaranteeing eventual success and fulfilment. For other downward branches from the life line, see travel lines on page 92. For rising branches, see page 34.

Branch from the life line curling in towards the thumb

A warning not to give up on life even if health, money or relationship problems look insurmountable.

See pages 31 and 33 for breaks and overlapping lines. An interpretation of diagonal lines crossing the life line, can be found on page 90. All these features can be timed using the life line timing chart on page 121.

Head line

Undoubtedly the most revealing of all the lines, the head line shows how you process information, articulate ideas and where your mental talents lie. Are you an intellectual, a businessperson or a creative type bursting with ideas? Do you prepare your ideas and words carefully or simply shoot from the hip?

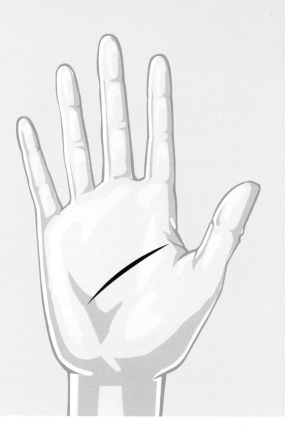

The head line will show how stress-prone you are, the extent to which you apply yourself to work, how quickly and efficiently you make decisions and how confident you are when articulating yourself. It is the most important and telling line of the hand when it comes to revealing aptitudes, talents and your particular type of intelligence and intellectual viewpoint. The left-hand head line will show your personal ideas of success and work, while on the right hand you can discover the ways in which you put these ideas into practice and utilize your gifts to achieve success in worldly terms. Professional success can often be most clearly shown in the right-hand head line.

Shape and form

The most variable of all the major lines, the head line can be curved, straight, long, short or broken. Ideally, its length should be consistent with the finger length (for example, short head line, short fingers). It can begin at any point in between the index finger or thumb and usually travels towards the outer edge of the palm, although it can end at almost any point in the palm away from the life line. When the line appears delicate, you can assess that your mentality is more fragile at present and that you should avoid too much stress. You may not be at your best in a crisis or in jobs that have punishing deadlines. When the line appears heavy or coarse, your mode of self-expression – personally (the left hand) or socially/professionally (the right hand) – may lack finesse. You may find that your attitude and way of solving problems is considered by others to be blunt, brusque and bullish. If the line is woolly, it indicates a woolly, vague and forgetful mind. Indecision is shown when the line splits into various strands at its end. It is important to exercise your mind and your memory.

Often the head lines on the left and right hands differ quite markedly, and this reveals an inconsistency between private/intimate (left) and public/work (right) roles. Perhaps the confidence level is markedly different, or in some ways you are two very different 'split' people.

Missing

When the head line is missing, this usually signifies that you have a Simian line (see page 68). On rare occasions, the head line will be absent in its entirety, but often there are some strands, however short or faint.

Remember, that because the head line is finely attuned to your way of thinking, your stress levels and mental health, it can fade out, strengthen or even change course slightly over time as you 'change your mind' and modify your way of dealing with your environment. It is the line most prone to changing its shape when you make direct changes to the way you approach and respond to life.

Duality

As with the other major lines, the head line can be read on more than one level at once. It not only discloses your actual thought processes, outlook and aptitudes but can also very tellingly reveal the actual events that shape your decisions and states of mind. (You will learn to time these events on page 122.)

Markings on the head line

Any marking, formation or crossing bar on this line will register the psychological changes in your mental attitudes to your personal and professional environments, as well as describing the sort of influence that different people have on your outlook, decisions and mental well-being. Sometimes the markings on the head line will accurately reveal actual physical changes taking place to your head or brain. Browse the following pages to identify the specific markings on your own hands.

Children's hands

In the hands of children it is not unusual to find head lines that are made up of a number of small interlinking lines. These can often resemble a chain or a series of little islands. This is especially common in those who have experienced a great deal of change or disruption in their immediate environment for the first six or seven years of their life. In most cases, these chains and islands will start to fade and eventually disappear as the child matures, develops and moves into adolescence.

Straight head line

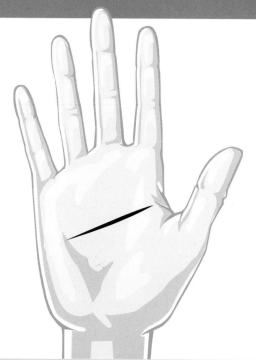

Work

At best, you have the cool, detached communication and reasoning skills that make you excellent in business and goal-orientated environments. With this head line, you are able to turn any creative talents you may have (as shown elsewhere in the hand) to your financial advantage, particularly when in partnership with others. The hand shape will confirm whether or not you are good with money, but this formation does show potential business acumen because there is a no-nonsense, practical approach and a determination to tackle projects logically and with cunning. You're good in a crisis because you are level-headed and rational.

Personality

You are perceptive, discerning and able to pick up information that escapes those who cannot 'read between the lines'. Add this to a tactical approach and a readiness to deal hands-on with everyday matters, and you have the key palm sign of sound judgement and practical common sense. (If your straight head line is fuzzy, wavy or in strands, you need to keep focused in order to be as productive with work and as clear-cut in your decision-making.) You have the temperament that questions everything. Only after being presented with concrete proof would you consider accepting another's opinion as fact. It is important for you to have the facts at your fingertips before making a decision.

Love

You look for equilibrium in all matters, particularly those relating to the heart. You are keen to spend much time exploring your feelings and digesting information before making relationship decisions. Partners may find it difficult to anticipate your moods or understand that you need time to process your feelings. Some would be surprised to learn that you can be very devious and manipulative when you put your mind to it. When interested in someone new, you systematically set out to win your prize. You would benefit from expressing your true feelings rather than bottling them up or expressing them with passive aggression.

Curved head line

Personality

People know where they stand with you. You are open, expressive and lay your cards on the table. You sometimes take this too far, however, and risk being tactless or undiplomatic. You are the type who wants to go with the flow, take calculated risks and explore new territory. For you, life is an adventure that could take a new twist any minute, and you want to be ready. You like things clear and simple and seek to find quick solutions to life's problems. Your creative instinct is strong; you pursue life and all kinds of relationships with infectious enthusiasm.

Work

You seek to work for yourself or be in an autonomous position in a company that offers opportunities to get ahead. Yet you may lose work to straight head line counterparts because you let your ideas be known and prefer not to play political games. Your instinct is not to get involved in the 'rat race' or be too focused on making money, preferring to have the freedom to explore creative avenues. You are motivated by the idea of producing a worthwhile end result. You would hate to be in an ambitious environment where you have to watch your back, but you like to win respect and recognition for your creative versatility.

Love

You love to surprise with presents, unexpected trips and spontaneous gestures. You are open to explore new ground sexually and dislike emotional games (particularly if your heart line is curved – see page 58). You are just as candid when expressing your relationship needs (unless your ring and middle fingers cling to each other – see pages 115). You are self-reliant and detached but not as practical as some and you would be just as happy to live on your own. Partners should respect your need for privacy and solitude, and must understand that you only share problems when you feel unable to cope on your own.

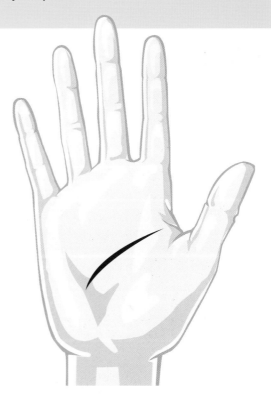

Deeply curved head line

Personality

You have enormous creative potential and probably immersed yourself in the world of the imagination from an early age. Whether you were day-dreaming at school or weaving intricate fantasies, you preferred to live in a world of make-believe. Now you do your best to avoid the harsh realities life throws your way, but you should not run away from commitments. There is a way forward without blaming others or avoiding responsibilities.

Work

In school, your approach to the world did not fit in with that of your peers, and it is likely that your education was minimal unless the subject sparked your imagination. In later life, you may carry a chip on your shoulder about not having the proper qualifications. Luckily, however, you are not really cut out for a highly competitive working environment. When there are opportunities to express creative freedom, your instinct may be to reject it. This is based on the fear that you won't be capable of hacking the routine or live up to the expectation of others. Or perhaps you are afraid of the burden of success?

Love

First, look to the type of heart line you have, as this will show your expectations and experiences in love. With your deeply curved head line, you are afraid of getting involved in any form of romantic liaison that could leave you exposed and vulnerable. You prefer the safety of your own secluded fantasy world. It's time to take stock, however, and realize that anyone capable of penetrating your defences and having creative pursuits in common deserves to be given a chance. You have so much to offer, and a vast reserve of love and affection to share with others, but will you let them in?

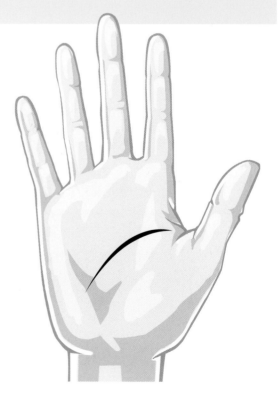

Short head line

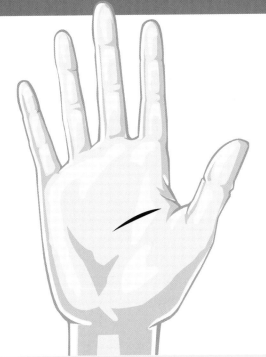

Love

It is likely that your heart line is longer than this line, suggesting you are ruled by your heart, not your head. You are driven by emotional responses and you tend to go with your gut reaction when your relationship encounters difficulties. You often don't think things through enough, preferring to remove yourself from the situation when the going gets tough. You also have a notoriously short fuse. Only later are you able to process what's been going on and digest the facts with objectivity. In general, you hate complications, but you create these when you act impetuously, often with little or no thought for the consequences.

Work

It is likely that you were good at only one or two subjects at school, but this does not mean you are incapable of having a good all-round knowledge in adulthood. You may look at those who possess long head lines and envy their versatility and ability to adapt themselves to new situations, but you are very much the specialist and need work that requires a specific talent. Your mind works best when dealing with one project at a time – this is because you have a short attention span and don't like distractions. You would do best to become an authority in one area, and could do well in any job that requires handling money.

Personality

This type of head line gives you the talent to grasp the essence of an idea quickly and confers a dislike of complexities, subtleties and red tape. You have the sort of mind that can process the basic facts quickly and your aim is to act incisively. Making decisions quickly (unless the head line is feathery or woolly – see page 37) comes naturally, but often you suffer as a result of not 'doing your homework'. You are best when you can apply yourself to a short-term situation. You are an impulsive person who likes to act on the spur of the moment; but watch a tendency to bolt from situations when the pressure's on or when there are delays to your plans.

Long head line

Personality

You process information slowly and carefully, mulling over the details and dissecting the various components involved, but you are versatile, have numerous interests and are able to handle many projects at once. One-to-one contact and talking things over with friends and colleagues is excellent therapy for you, as you depend upon feedback and two-way exchange. You hate to be pushed into making quick decisions – you are afraid to miss a subtle but important point. Your thoughts flow most freely when there is no pressure from deadlines.

Work

You have lots of ambitious plans but which one are you going to tackle first? It is important to organize your schedule and focus on long-term projects that can be developed. A natural strategist, you have the patience to plan and see projects through to completion. You know that success comes from preparation, attention to detail and reading the small print. You may have a love of words and enjoy teaching and writing. Others rarely get anything less than a well-thought-out reply to any questions. Since you are probably well-read and consider yourself a student of life, you are able to bring a diverse range of experiences to any job you tackle.

Love

You are a thinker who carefully considers your road ahead as well as any alternative routes, but partners may not know where they stand because you tend to over-analyse relationship dilemmas and appear to procrastinate endlessly. Will you stay or will you move on to new pastures? You don't attempt to make decisions until you have all the facts at your fingertips, and even then too much information may delay the process further. Nevertheless, partners need to have all their facts ready if they start an argument with you or try to hurry you on – you are the type who will pull out a list of reasons why you need a little more time to make up your mind.

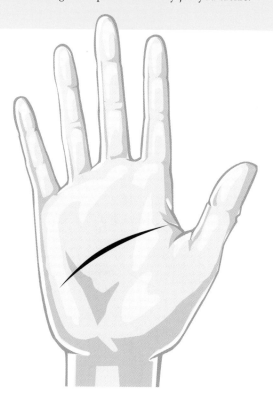

Head line commencing near thumb

Love

This can be a tough head line to have when in relationships. You are often rather tense and keyed up, so you find it difficult to relax with loved ones. Look to the shape and ending of the heart line (particularly on the left hand) to see how you can best express yourself emotionally. If friendships get in the way of personal plans, resist the impulse to cast them aside ruthlessly. You should be aware of your explosive temper and stubborn resistance to accepting others' ideas and help.

Work

You are not one to bother with the fine details (particularly if you have short fingers or a short head line). You are excellent at identifying the heart of any matter and tackling problems head on, but be careful not to miss the subtleties of a situation. Others can benefit from your no-nonsense, energetic approach. You will be considered an asset in any company that hires you to do battle on their behalf, as long as they are not in the firing line. You may need to take extended periods of time off work to unwind and disengage from work stresses. If this is impossible, see to it that you channel your aggression into sport.

Personality

This head line gives you a personal style that is combative, courageous and dynamic. You are impatient and irritable but strong-willed and focused on achieving your aims. Your general attitude is to attack first and ask questions later. Subtlety is not your strong point and you are not out to win fans, either. If you are determined to ride roughshod over the opposition, then at least pay close attention to your health, as you are very stress-prone. Your pugnacious approach to life can antagonize others and provoke more opposition than is necessary. In fact, others may go out of their way to ensure you don't get what you want because of your bellicose manner. You seem to want to argue the toss every time.

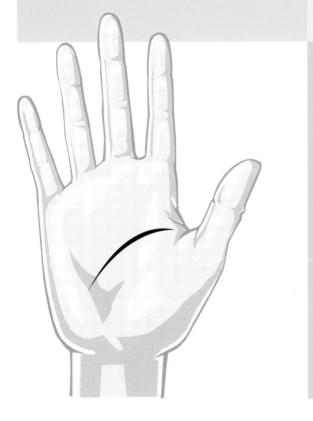

Head line commencing near index finger

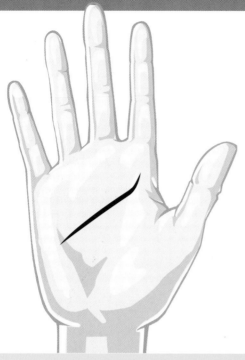

Work

It is likely that you had a desire at some stage to express yourself in one of the performing arts. You are suited to work that requires winning accounts and bringing in clients – work that makes full use of your ability to promote yourself or a product. You assume that positions of authority are yours for the taking, but there may be times in your working life when your plans are thwarted because of your arrogance or lack of training. You have many ambitions to succeed (particularly when this line is on your right hand) but must learn the ropes and some humility before earning your place at the top.

Love

One of your greatest talents is your ability to charm others. You seek out a partner who looks good on your arm but who won't have the charisma to outshine you. Your persuasive, self-confident manner attracts partners, but many are surprised to find that your self-assurance is bravado. With luck, you will meet a partner who wants to have an equal relationship with you, and this will curb your natural instinct to dominate or subjugate. This tyrannical streak of yours may see you encounter a clash of wills when a loved one does not accept your opinion as gospel.

Personality

You emit an imperious air of supreme confidence – some might say cockiness – and believe in the power and authority of your words. It is likely that you were brought up convinced you were the centre of the universe, and you grew up expecting the world to share your inflated opinion of yourself. You have big ambitions, dramatic flair, set high goals for yourself and have a manner that commands respect. At best, you have an enterprising, generous and philanthropic nature and there is the potential to be influential and inspirational but you must resist the urge to exert a Svengali-like control over followers.

Break in head line

Starting over

Breaks always signal the end of a chapter in your life. Look to determine whether the break is on the left (private self) or right hand (public self). When the first line comes to an end (the exact age can be timed using the head line timing chart on page 122), there is an end to a way of thinking or behaving. Very often, there is a definite break in routine or life path. Occasionally, this is due to a physical injury or shock (usually – although not always – to the head), but usually this change occurs because of a divorce, a parting of the ways, the death of a loved one or being 'born again'. The event will have set you on a different course with a new attitude and different priorities.

The strength and clarity of the new line will determine how strong, effective and resilient this new outlook of yours will be.

Sometimes the new line will emerge from the direction of the index finger, pointing to a new-found confidence in yourself, a spiritual rebirth or entering a position of greater control in your life. On other hands, the new line appears below the original and this implies that you have taken on a outlook that focuses on your inner self and the impulse is to withdraw from public life. Your main objective is to live your life for yourself rather than trying to please others around you.

Overlaps

Often the head lines will overlap and this shows a gradual coming to terms with the change in routine and making a slow move towards a new life. Look to see whether the overlapping lines are protected by a square (see page 82), suggesting the transition is smoother because of a constant in your life at that time. When the lines do not overlap, a break away from recent stresses must be made in order to take stock and regroup.

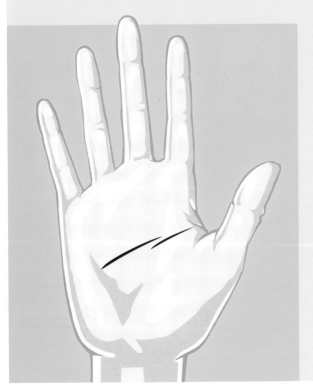

Head line with additional branch

Work

Your mentality is highly adaptable – you are capable of processing fresh ideas and learning new subjects very quickly. Whether it is learning a different language in six weeks or picking up a complicated knitting pattern, you are able to grasp the essentials of any subject that interests you and then apply this to suit your own needs. You may be blessed with an exceptional memory and have ingenious ways of working. Others are amazed at how self-motivated, driven and ambitious you are. This approach is a blessing, so aim to work in an area that brings you enormous pleasure.

Love

With all this creative talent and potential for success professionally, your personal life may have its fair share of practical difficulties that demand you make choices. You are ambitious to succeed and need a partner who also wants to push forward and achieve results, otherwise you will lose respect for them. Often, though, the temptation is to get involved with someone who is steadfast, conservative and rather boring. Sometimes a partner feels they are taking second place to your many creative outlets so, if you are ready to commit, either work with them or adapt your hectic life to make room for a relationship.

Personality

You are gifted with mental dexterity and are driven to apply your ample creative talents. You will never be bored and cannot understand those who are. For you, life offers endless choices and your biggest worry is whether you will be able to fit everything in. When the head line is curved, you are motivated to express yourself in a dramatic way, such as performing or interior design. You take risks when opportunity knocks. It may be hard to earn a living from your talents because you need to learn to value yourself. If the branch appears on a straight head line, though, you have learned to utilize your talents in a practical form. You have inventive ways of bringing business to your door.

Two separate head lines

Work

You are the ultimate promoter, publicist or fundraiser, and are keenly aware of how others see you. You are highly intelligent and very capable, if not slightly unpredictable. Colleagues will soon discover that the person who is articulate, confident and authoritative is also the person in private who is insecure, painfully shy and self-doubting. Some of you may even have a 'secret life' that few know about.

Personality

Two head lines reveal a dual personality, each half struggling for dominance. Usually one of them begins near the index finger and seeps majestically into the hand, while the other is tied to the life line and is much shorter. This suggests that one part of you is an outgoing, fun character that thrives on taking chances, starting new ventures and involving people in your life. The other is a withdrawn, sombre soul who is distrustful and even a little paranoid and suspicious of others' motives. This combination can produce a rather neurotic personality that is intensely private yet driven to be out front, centre stage.

Love

Often the more self-confident side of you is expressed through work, and the insecure worrier is revealed to those closest to you (regardless of whether these head lines are on your right or left hand). Two head lines point to someone supremely capable in many areas of life but who is perhaps rather ingenuous, demanding and childish in relationships. There is a gulf between how you perceive yourself in public and in private and how you manage these sides. Potential partners may be attracted to the enigmatic, all-coping public image you project but may discover a very different person behind closed doors. The key is in integrating both sides into your personal life.

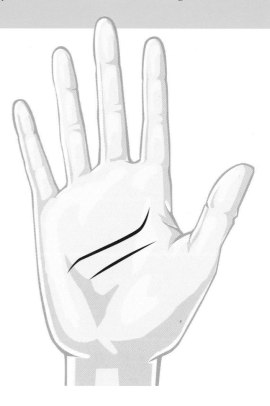

Forked head line

Small fork

Known as the 'Writer's Fork', this marking is a sign of a keen intellect and astute mind. You are always seeking knowledge and picking up facts, and are quick to grasp the gist of most subjects. You pride yourself on an open-minded approach to life and can analyse matters objectively and clearly. You are also pretty versatile and resourceful, and have a variety of interests. You have the ability to understand and debate both sides of an argument – if someone is stating one strong view, you feel compelled to counter it with an alternative standpoint. This makes you a good mediator, analyst and teacher who can offer practical solutions to creative problems or offer a creative approach to a practical matter.

If the head line is clear or unusually formed, too, there will be a talent for writing. If your head line is curved (see page 39), you should consider writing from your imagination. With a straight head line (see page 38), you will prefer writing from your own experience.

A small fork at the end of the head line (as shown to the right) suggests good analytical powers and an enquiring mind.

Large fork

With this feature, there is a tendency to go off the rails or become addicted to crises. Sometimes it is a sign of a literal split in your life – in childhood there may have been a parental split and later in life you chose (or were forced) to break ties in a close relationship. It is usually an either/or decision – you could have continued down the same path but, in diverting from it, you have created a double life (and a lot of 'baggage') that is difficult to sustain. A potentially self-destructive feature in your hand, it reveals a tendency to react to life in an unpredictable and wilful manner. Often this large fork symbolizes an internal personality split – at worst there is little ability to rationalize and often extreme emotions are expressed without much self-control.

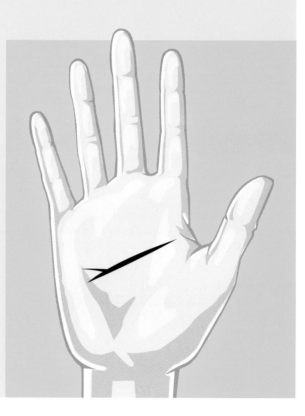

Signs of depression

Head line that humps up under the middle finger

(a) This suggests sudden inexplicable mood swings and depression, both of which may be due to hormonal imbalances. Although this feature (particularly with a long ring finger) suggests a temperament prone to depression, its position on the hand indicates that the major shift in attitude will occur in the early to late 30s due to a specific event. (Remember that the major lines show character traits and can be timed to show when these traits are triggered off by a major life event.)

Fine sloping lines descending from the head line

(b) This is not as long-term as (a) but the effects will be felt all the same. They indicate short periods when events take their toll and you feel stressed and disheartened. These sloping lines must fall from the head line to qualify, and each one can be timed. To make an accurate assessment as to when depression is most likely to occur, refer to the head line timing chart on page 122.

Curved head line descending under the middle finger

(c) When the line dives down, you are so sensitive to hurt that you may desire to lose yourself in a fantasy world, escaping from the harsh realities around you. You may get easily depressed but must share these feelings with loved ones who can give you a clearer perspective on matters. At best you may have an artistic talent and be highly creative

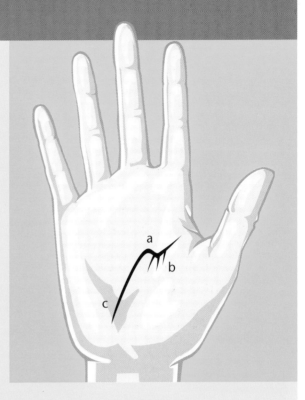

and visually minded, but don't invest all your dreams in one goal – have a back-up plan. You may, at some point, have a fear of losing your sanity (particularly if there is a star on your head line). Luckily, however, with this type of head line there is often an additional branch lying horizontally across the hand. This provides a degree of balance, reason and level-headedness to the personality and enables you to have the best of both worlds. You can function well in the 'real' world while tapping into your creative imagination and utilizing these gifts in a practical manner. Read the profile on page 40 for further personality traits. An island in the head line (see page 51) is another sign of depression.

Branches rising from head line

To be genuine, these branches must rise out from the head line rather than cross through it, otherwise they could be part of the health line (see page 91), a relationship line (see pages 93–4) or a simple crossing line (see page 51). These branches can be timed using the head line timing chart on page 122.

Towards the index finger

You wish to contribute work that is substantial, and desire to be an authority in a specialist area. This line shows increasing intellectual confidence from the age it hits the head line. You may feel more able to articulate ideas from this time on, whether it is in front of an audience or at work. It is often a period of results, when something special is achieved using your intellectual talents (such as having a book published or a project coming to fruition).

Towards the middle finger

The age at which this branch touches your head line is the time when you take on more personal (left hand) or professional (right hand) responsibilities. Perhaps the focus is on a home or business investment or developing a project that requires planning and dedication. If the head line weakens, breaks or forms an island after this marking, it suggests that the responsibility may be stressful.

Towards the ring finger

When the branch rises from the head line, it indicates the beginning of a period of creative pursuits as well as acclaim for projects completed at this time.

Towards the little finger

You have ambitions to be shrewd in business and possess good negotiating skills (particularly with a straight head line). It is a sign of strong earning potential. The time it emerges from the head line signifies a period when you focus on earning more money or perhaps invest in a training course to broaden your skills. If positioned at the end of the line and of the same length as the remainder of the head line, this is a Writer's Fork (see page 48).

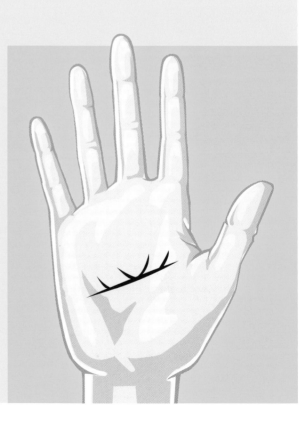

Other features on head line

As with all markings, don't forget to check whether the line improves or weakens after the marking. This will show whether the effect has the potential to be positive or negative.

Dot or dots on the line

This shows a short period of worry or tension, or it may indicate the possibility of a blow to the head. When there is a series of dots, it is likely that you suffer from headaches or migraines.

Crossing lines

These warn that others may try to interfere in your plans. They also show general obstacles that you may encounter, plus some stress and worry.

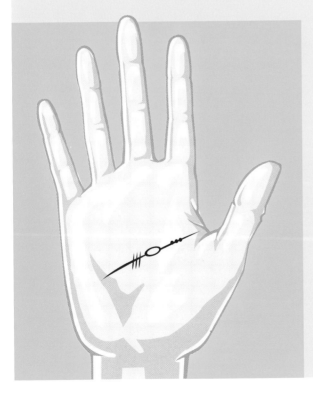

Island

One of the most fascinating of the markings found on hands, the island is aptly named because with this formation you feel isolated and lonely as though left fending for yourself on a desert island. An island anywhere on the hand can show feelings of isolation, stress, sensitivity, dissociation, loneliness, remoteness or withdrawal. As with major markings, it can be read in two ways: as a personality trait you possess and/or an event that brings this personality trait to the surface. For example, on the head line, you may be naturally stress-prone and sensitive, as well as experience periods of stress, mental fatigue, self-doubt or negativity at a particular point in your life (see the head line timing chart on page 122).

On the head line this island will affect your intellect and thought processes, suggesting your ability to reason and communicate is coloured by stress, isolation and so on. As is often the case, an island here can show a greater mental sensitivity to external circumstances. You should avoid stressful situations where there is a great deal of pressure to commit or fulfil obligations. Working in a job where there are regular stressful deadlines or being in a possessive, controlling relationship would be harmful to your mental health. Your reaction may be to withdraw, to cut yourself off or to suffer a breakdown. Instead, you should seek to clarify and address the situation and then put it into perspective. In extreme cases, there are large islands (plus interruptions on the fate and life lines) on those who have had major breakdowns or periods of depression and detachment. For other signs, see page 49.

An island is the proverbial Achilles' heel – the weak spot that still has the potential to create something outstanding out of a stressful period of soul-searching. It should come as no surprise that an island here is also a key sign of intelligence, perhaps because the intellect is so sensitive, and with it you are more insightful and contemplative than most.

The marking can be an upper, lower or central island. The upper island (when the formation sits on top of the head line) indicates stress from professional circumstances. The lower island relates to personal problems, while the central island (where the head line runs around either side of the formation) is more significant, suggesting a great sensitivity and stress from all areas of life. With all islands, the energy flow of the head line is interrupted, indicating that your mental energy is divided and sapped, leaving you feeling low on motivation and mental courage.

Star on the line

This marking has a twofold interpretation. First, you have an approach to life that stimulates others and are attractive company, able to entertain with scintillating conversation. If there are other markings of success on the head, fate or Apollo lines, a star on the head line can indicate creative brilliance – the potential to produce something

exceptional. With a star (particularly when this is sitting on the line, rather than cutting through it), success is likely to be unexpected and perhaps somewhat unsettling.

Second, if other factors in the hands concur, a star formation can point to high blood pressure and is sometimes found on those who have had strokes (although a star on the head line is by no means a definite sign that you will suffer a stroke). If there is some physical shock that has taken place at the time of the star (see the head line timing chart on page 122), this is often due to a prolonged build-up of tension, or perhaps not being able to release your anger appropriately.

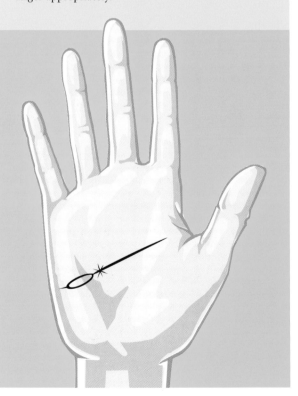

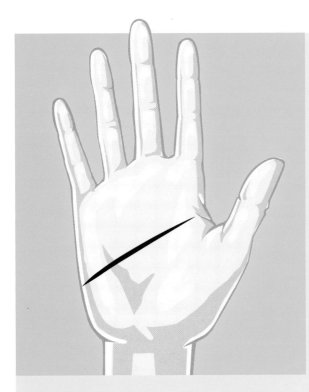

prescriptions if necessary. If there are worries about your eyesight, a medical opinion, of course, should be sought first.

In psychological terms, a head line that ends in an eye-shape formation may suggest a rather blinkered or short-sighted approach to other people's views. You may have developed a way of blocking out the opinions of others and could also have settled for a rather dogmatic approach to any problem solving that you encounter. This meaning could be applied to either your personal life (if found on the left hand) or to your professional and social situation (if found on the right hand).

The Sydney line

This is a straight line that extends to the outer edge of the palm. Please note that the heart line will always be present.

Discovered by medical researchers in Australia, this line has been linked to hyperactivity and restlessness, particularly when found in children. Researchers have found this type of head line on those children who experienced learning difficulties that may have caused delays or other disruption to their education.

See page 45 for a break in the head line, overlapping head lines and a square on the overlap. See page 49 for sloping hair lines off the head line, and page 50 for hair lines rising off the head line.

Due to the star's explosive nature, any physical ailment or success from the intellect is most likely to come 'out of the blue'. Yet an unexpected event can sometimes leave its owner feeling victimized, delicate or afraid of a repeat situation. It is a sign of being highly attuned and of having a nervous disposition, particularly when there are many lines on the hand.

Ending in an eye-shape

This marking can develop when there is a weakness in one of the eyes (left hand marking = left eye; right hand = right eye). If this appears in either of your hands, it should not be a particularly alarming discovery but it may be worth considering having a eye test, so that you can get glasses or change

Relationship between head and life lines

Head line lightly joined to life line

This shows a balanced approach to life, with a healthy amount of self-confidence, caution and independence. You are clever enough to listen to others' advice, yet independent enough to take chances and take responsibility for the choices you make.

Head line independent from life line

You have always been encouraged to have your own mind and to express ideas, even if they differed from those of friends and family. (Your level of confidence as well as the potential to make a success of your talents can be best seen in the shape and course of the head line, as well as other factors such as finger length and fingerprint patterns.) Perhaps your parents had too much to do, and so you learned to look after yourself, play on your own and develop your own set of rules.

You have a reckless, impulsive streak (particularly if you have a long ring finger) so it is vital that you learn to take responsibility for your actions. You don't want to be held back and you will take risks if they have the potential to take you on a new path.

The most important aspect here is that there is an uncompromising need to direct your own life – sooner or later. When the fate line is tied to the life line (see page 77) or the life line is chained or feathery (see page 29), it may take longer to assert

yourself and to stop relying on the opinions of family or partners. Nevertheless the search for independence is a major life challenge. If you have this head/life line relationship on a water hand (see page 21), you may, at first, cling to partners for security and an identity, until one day you decide to break free from this. Your sudden, emotionally driven response to seek independence often results in a big drama and relationship crisis, although by asserting yourself you will have a stronger sense of your own individuality.

If this occurs on other hand shapes, you may display a marked talent for business (earth hand), promotion (fire hand) or working in the media (air hand).

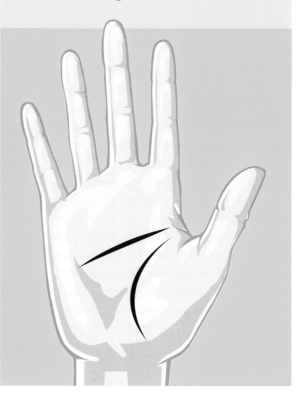

Head line closely tied to life line

Although you may have been intellectually advanced beyond your years, your upbringing caused some delay in your emotional independence or sexual development. Perhaps you were held back when young because of a lack of opportunity or because the family situation was stifling or restrictive. Maybe family members took it upon themselves to run your life. With this formation, you were at times quite happy to let them. If this head/life line relationship is accompanied by a late-starting fate line (see page 76), you found your niche later in life after breaking away from early restrictions. Even if there was an absence of parental control, you gave the impression of needing to be looked after and continue to do so! At times, you can be withdrawn, pessimistic and lacking in confidence. At worst, you want others to make the decisions, abdicating responsibility and being afraid to take chances. Your cautious approach suggests to partners that you don't want to commit. They may demand that you be less co-dependent, make the first move and take responsibility for decisions that affect the relationship.

Head line beginning in the palm centre

Others see you as detached and sometimes rather uncaring. This may not be how you wish to be perceived, but you are very self-protective and do not want people invading your space. You will go to extreme lengths to maintain your privacy and keep your personal secrets. Many of you prefer to live alone and your response, when feeling invaded, may be to hurt or attack others. It is not uncommon for you to be abrupt and rude if you feel intruded upon. Some of you may have experienced a family event or personality clash at home during your early life that forced you to protect yourself by detaching and seeking independence elsewhere. Later, you built up a life and routine away from these early ties. On the positive side, by preferring to separate yourself from the demands and opinions of others, you are free to be objective and independent, and these traits benefit you in your chosen work.

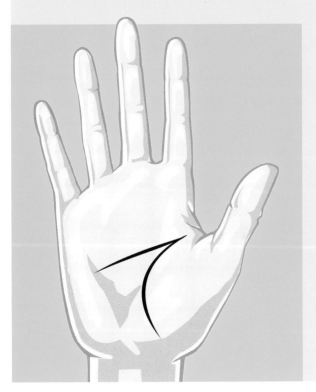

Heart line

What do you expect from a partner and from relationships in general? What traits are brought to the fore in relationships and sex? The heart line reveals your emotional and sexual responses, patterns of behaviour, needs and expectations. The heart line on the left hand governs all intensely personal feelings, experiences and behaviour from childhood. The right heart line says much about how you see yourself as a lover, partner or a hopeful on the dating scene, as well as how your sexuality is practised and experienced on a physical level.

The heart line will tell you how you begin and end relationships, how you tackle emotional and sexual problems, and the type of problems you have in partnerships. These partnerships can be sexual or platonic. It reveals how you relate to others on an emotional, feeling level (the head line will disclose how you are on a mental, rational level). The heart line is the prime indicator of your emotional and sexual make-up.

Shape and form

Most heart lines consist of a short series of interwoven lines, resembling a chain of small links. In addition, they often feature branches, island formations and crossing lines. This suggests a healthy measure of emotion and vulnerability. The heart line usually ends in a small fork underneath the index and middle fingers, showing a balance between realism (middle finger) and idealism (index) in relationships but a need for honest and regular communication. When it is too delicate, there can be hypersensitivity.

There are two further points to consider when examining the shape of the heart line. First, a complex-looking heart line will reveal a complex set of emotional–sexual responses. Second, an unmarked or evenly laid out heart line will reveal emotional coolness or a difficulty in feeling empathy or passion.

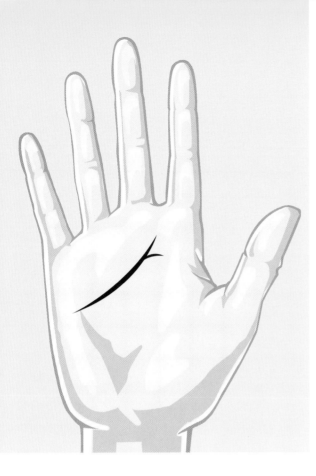

Missing and doubled-up

Occasionally the heart line is missing, and more often than not this is due to the presence of a Simian line (see page 68). Sometimes there appears to be a doubling-up of the heart line (ensure this is not mistaken for the girdle of Venus – see page 88). When this is present, the heart line takes on enormous importance. Both lines should be assessed carefully.

Duality

Although not a reliable indicator of events and exact dates of events, the heart line can still be read on two levels. It reveals both your psychological attitudes to love, sex and relating and the actual course your love life takes. This major palm line also shows any physical developments connected to the heart and lungs.

Markings on the heart line

Most markings on this line should not be read independently, as they all contribute to the overall course and flow of the heart line, which will be interpreted in this section. Important additional and unusual markings are, however, explained on pages 64–5.

Relating

The heart line won't necessarily reveal your relationship history. Rather it shows your reactions towards relating. Does your heart rule your head? It may do, if the heart line is longer or deeper than the head line on the left hand. When longer on the right hand, you may 'wear your heart on your sleeve' and emotions may influence your decisions.

Children's hands

There is usually a noticeable change in the heart line when a child reaches puberty. As they become aware of their sexuality and their emotional needs, a teenager's heart line will develop accordingly. Internal and external events in adolescence will shape the line. Before adolescence, the heart line is more likely to show their potential in relating as an adult, as well as how they are currently relating to their parents and siblings (left hand) and to friends (right hand). It will reveal details such as sibling rivalry, a caring nature and jealousy.

Straight and curved heart lines

If you are unsure whether the heart line is curved or straight, place a ruler from the beginning of the heart line to its end. Sometimes heart lines end with numerous branches. Take the most dominant branch continuing in the direction of the main line.

Usually, couples in long-term relationships will have similar heart lines. For example, a curved heart line is often seen on couples who share a strong domestic streak. If couples have very different heart lines, this can lead to an acceptance of the fundamental differences in their approaches.

The following characteristics are a little exaggerated, in order to highlight the basic differences.

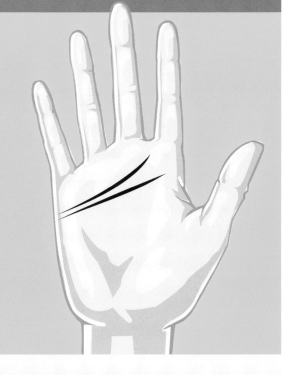

Straight

- Emotionally reserved, introverted
- Controlled, thoughtful and analytical
- Looks for sincere, earnest long-term mates
- Seeks emotional and mental compatibility
- Seeks a meeting of minds
- Will often wait for signs of interest
- Wants equality and a supportive union
- Expressive via words and memories
- Sex will bond, unite and reassure
- Sometimes inhibited and afraid to ask
- Dislikes discord, tension or unpredictability
- Employs emotional blackmail, passive aggression or suffers in silence

Curved

- Emotionally demonstrative, extroverted
- Spontaneous and enthusiastic
- Looks for attractive, daring mates
- Seeks physical and sexual chemistry
- Seeks fun and adventure
- Will initiate contact
- Wants to conquer, dominate and win
- Expressive via presents and surprises
- Sex empowers and releases tension
- Often exhibitionistic and wants too much
- Dislikes stale or predictable situations
- Hot-tempered, acts rashly, quits the relationship and then makes up

Curved heart line to index finger

Personality

You are demonstrative and warm, able to put people at ease and make them feel the most important person in the room. Yet giving 100 percent of yourself to others sets you up for disappointment when most don't reciprocate as fully. You tend to put friends, family and lovers on a pedestal and are genuinely hurt when they fall off – you seem to forget that they are human and most are not as generous with time and money as you are. The fact is that others can't live up to your expectations. Perhaps you do so much for others because you yearn for the same in return.

Work

You are a generous colleague who is the first to offer workmates a shoulder to cry on. Your positive, spontaneous nature and infectious optimism can inspire others in work and in love, and you could find a professional role to this end (as long as you know you can only inspire them, not change them). You work hard to win friends by being overly generous and supportive, but you feel rejected when you realize that many colleagues won't go the distance for you. Your toughest challenge is to give as much as you want to, but to do so without the expectation of anything in return.

Love

Others may accuse you of looking at life through rose-tinted glasses, but you know that you are simply an idealist. You long for – or to be – the knight in shining armour and know that settling for second best is tantamount to defeat. You swing from feeling that your closest relationship works well to wondering why there seems to be 'something missing'. You become angry when others don't exhibit the same level of devotion and when there are signs that a relationship is not 'perfect'. In fact your expectations are too high – apparently partners need to be superhuman psychics, first to know what you want and second to fill any voids you may have. Invest in yourself rather than looking for a partner to reinforce these feelings.

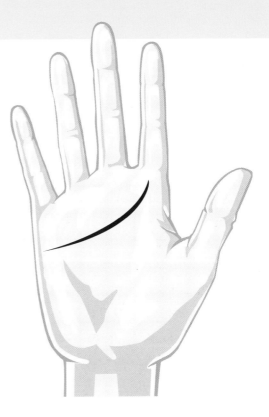

Curved heart line to middle finger

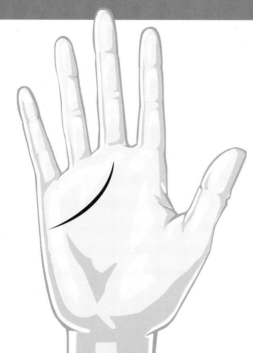

Love

Yours is a strong sexual nature, interested in extremes. You enjoy the chase, the sparks of sexual chemistry and the pursuit of physical pleasure. Partners may be scared off by your intensity and insatiable need to experience everything physically, and at the same time may feel you are 'unreal' because you never seem to let your emotional guard down. You have learned to avert their interest in the real you by attracting them sexually. For you, an emotionally satisfying union will require trust and risking exposure of the real you behind the façade.

Personality

Who are you? Are you really the person that everyone around you encounters, or is it just a façade? You fear that if you drop your mask others will see your faults and 'ordinariness' that are so apparent to you when you look at yourself. This mask is also one of self-protection against being hurt by emotional ties – something you were not able to protect yourself against when younger. Putting up a brick wall keeps out those wanting to pry into your soul. With this heart line formation, there is a quest to reinvent yourself and you may try on various masks along the way to see which fits best.

Work

You may find yourself attracted to work that requires playing a role very different to your true self. Or perhaps, through playing someone else, you will be on your way to understanding your real personality. The obvious choice may be acting, where you can draw from your experiences but project a different character to an audience. (Signs of acting talent and success can be found by examining the head line, the shape of the ring finger and whorls on the fingertips.) Many of you, though, may resist the intimate exposure and soul-bearing demanded by acting and feel drawn to professional situations in which you can hide behind a front, or be incognito.

Straight heart line ending below index

Personality

In life, you are able to balance idealism with a practical approach to personal and professional commitments. Although you want to believe the best of everyone, you accept that relationships of all kinds require nurturing, support and hard work. You have an adult and long-term view of life – so it will come as no surprise that you value reliability and honesty in others, and honour the commitments you make personally.

Work

As dedicated in your work as you are to personal commitments, you strike a good balance between practical application and hopeful optimism. You are a valuable ally and dependable support system to colleagues. Yet why are you sometimes overlooked for promotion? You are shrewd and considered in your approach, but you are not so good at asking for things for yourself. Ensure that your needs in the workplace are met.

Love

You tend to be very analytical and often spend time questioning your feelings and those of your partner. A lover can't make any comment without it being processed and analysed. A good judge of character, you nevertheless tend to be too harsh a critic in love. You look for many signals from a prospective partner before committing yourself and have a mental checklist of characteristics they must have to qualify. Sometimes, though, once you have dissected and investigated a situation, you are afraid to express yourself. You should avoid suffering in silence or playing emotional games. When there are problems, learn to tackle them head on and express your needs and desires clearly.

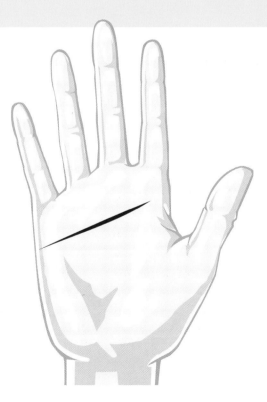

Straight, short heart line

Work

This challenging heart line faces some potential difficulties in the workplace, too. A sensitive soul like you can sometimes fall victim to office politics or gossip because your instinct is to reveal too much of yourself in order to win friends. After a while, though, you learn that clamming up not only protects your position but also gives you control over your environment. You may turn to helping others, maybe as a counsellor or advisor, as you can then empathize with others while healing your own wounds.

Love

Will sex lead to love? Although you may find yourself seeking sexual contact to form a bond with another, deep down you would prefer to do this through expressing emotions and ideas, but are afraid of exposing your vulnerability. The easy way out would be to operate on a purely sexual level and hope that this fulfils your needs for contact and companionship. The honest way would be to explore emotional depths with a loved one capable of doing this, and let this lead to a sexual union based on a meeting of minds, trust and shared goals. Stop calling yourself a pragmatist in love and have the courage to dive in at the deep end.

Personality

Forgetting the past is a great deal harder for you than for most. You carry a somewhat cynical attitude to life and relationships that may be justified, but it certainly does you little good. Past hurts, let-downs and insecurities resurface when you find yourself attracted to someone new. Your instinct is to protect yourself by hiding your vulnerability beneath a tough, caustic armour of sharp-tongued responses or streetwise defensiveness. Or you may be so focused on having your own needs met this time that you neglect your partner's needs. Either of these responses provokes the sort of negative response you were cynically expecting. Why seek love and friendship by courting rejection?

High-set and low-set heart lines

Most heart lines are set a good distance from the base of the fingers, but sometimes the line is either placed higher up or set significantly lower, nearer the head line. The following will not apply to anyone who has a Simian or semi-Simian line (see page 68).

High-set

Often you are too wrapped up in yourself to genuinely empathize with someone else. If you do find time to listen, your response is to compare it to one of your own experiences. Sometimes you might say: 'That's enough about me. Let's talk about you. So, what do you think of me?' You may fall into the category of the incessant head-nodder – the type you often see interviewing people on TV who is too busy mentally preparing the next question – or perhaps the type who can top any tale of woe with a personal story.

When your index finger is long, you put yourself in the other person's place long enough to give them advice on how to run their lives effectively. Everything would be fine if they would follow your suggestions! With a long ring finger, though, you would like to be seen to help, but you would really rather get off the phone and call someone who will be happy to hear all about you instead.

Low-set

You are a good listener, someone who can relate to others' problems and offer practical advice and support. In this case, the heart line is closer to the head line, suggesting an ability to provide constructive feedback and sympathy. Although focused on your own life, you are able to help others by drawing on your own intense experiences. If your index finger is long, you will empathize but won't let others cry on your shoulder for too long. You will want to see proof that they are picking themselves up and moving on. You are a firm believer in encouraging others to be self-determining and have no time for self-pity. If the ring finger is dominant, you will let them wallow and be happy to throw in a few of your own hard-luck stories.

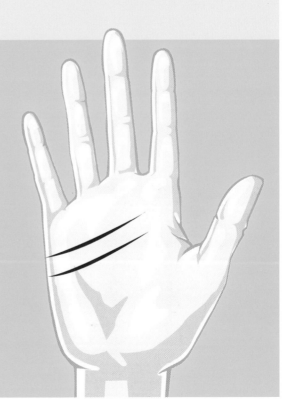

Other features on heart line

Remember to assess whether these markings appear on the left hand (which reveals deep-rooted emotional needs) or the right hand (which shows the trials and tribulations of dating, flirting, mixing and socializing).

Island in the heart line

These are common on heart lines, particularly under the ring and little fingers and show the adjustments that you must make during relationships. There are usually fewer islands later in the heart line (towards the index finger), and perhaps this suggests you grow more comfortable with yourself as you grow older. The fact that so many palms have major islands (or indeed a chain of islands) on the heart line suggests that relationships can often bring out your insecurities, and in so doing, force you to compromise and work hard to keep the union strong.

When a long, well-formed island follows a sloping branch off the heart line, this can show difficulties in adjusting after the break-up of a relationship. (All short, sloping branch lines at the early to middle stages of the heart line show difficulties or endings.) An island following a relationship break-up can show the long process of learning to trust again.

Arrows at the start of the heart line

These interesting marks are signs of jealousy – not just the green-eyed type but, at worst, the more unpleasant, spiky, prickly, sharp-tongued, resentful sorts. You may be notoriously self-protective, too. You should recognize a destructive side in you that is unforgiving and unwilling (or unable) to put aside past hurts.

Descending, hook-like branch

This sign, which does not touch the life or head line (see page 66), shows that there was a difficulty in understanding your sexuality in early adolescence. Perhaps there was confusion or non-acceptance of your own sexual feelings or perception. When found on the left hand, this is a deep-rooted concern. When on the right hand, it is particularly important for you to search for like-minded people and explore your feelings in the open. This is not necessarily a

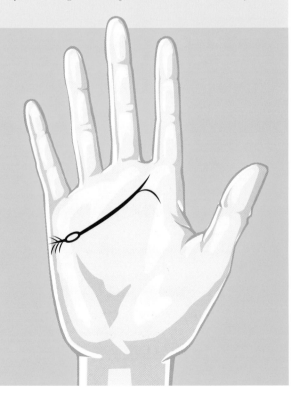

sign of homosexuality. What it does show is some doubt and insecurity over your sexual identity and desires, whether you are same-sex-orientated or not. One can speculate that, if found only on the left, such doubts may remain private, concealed or repressed. When only on the right hand, it may be a factor later brought out into the open (and explored) by socialization.

Complete break with new heart line

Usually the break is a minor one that occurs at the beginning of the heart line, under the little finger, and this shows an adjustment to your sexuality or relationship needs when young because of an early experience. A more complete break is a rare, but very noticeable, formation. It can show the breakdown of a relationship that, when strong, seemed to define who you really were. The loss of this 'soul mate' prompts an emotional overhaul, with you desperate to re-evaluate your emotional needs and responses. You may question what brought you to the brink of despair. Along with reckless, impulsive signs in the hand, this feature warns of self-destructive behaviour in relationships – throwing an existing, stable relationship to one side while galloping into a passionate, all-consuming romance that may fizzle out soon afterwards. You may appear to lose all reason as you venture forth to explore a romantic and/or sexual tryst. If this fails, the instinct may be to try to pick up the pieces or find a new, safer option, which may not initially seem to be as personally satisfying.

Straight heart line extending across the hand

To be genuine, this line must extend to beyond the middle of the index finger towards the edge of the palm. It is the sign of the person who usually puts work before relationships. This is often called the humanitarian heart line, but I suspect these qualities, even if present, are at the expense of one-to-one relationships. Sometimes this is due to self-centredness and an unwillingness to share your life with someone, but most often this line indicates trouble coming to terms with your emotional needs.

You prefer to live in your head and avoid complex feelings. There may be a fundamentally selfish quality, particularly if the hand shape or head line show a materialistic character. You adopt an either/or view of relationships and work, and the latter is usually the more seductive. You may meet partners – usually a fellow workaholic – through work or later develop a working partnership together that drives and steers the personal relationship. In fact, it may often be the only thing still standing after the dust settles in emotional disputes.

You should avoid channelling your passion, energy and creativity into career pursuits at the expense of a personal life and good working relationships. The humanitarian qualities in you may come out as you feel a need to use your social conscience – the need to fight for a cause, fundraise or work towards some other altruistic goal – but what's left on the one-to-one level when you arrive home?

Heart line descending into life line

Personality

Most people are sensitive souls but often insensitive to the feelings of others. You, however, are highly sensitive and vulnerable but are also able to empathize and offer the right kind of support. Your early experiences have made you acutely sensitive to rejection, criticism and hurt, but they have also provided you with the tools to help others gain understanding. As for yourself, at worst you could cut yourself off from the hurt of rejection by refusing to trust again. Why risk giving so much and being hurt again? For you, however, life will always be richer for having dared to love and risked being hurt.

Work

Your compassionate nature makes you a natural in the helping professions, particularly if you have the Ring of Solomon or medical stigmata (see pages 88–9). Counselling, support groups or an advice bureau would benefit from your understanding of grief and loss – but you can only be of genuine help if you have moved on from feeling victimized by a past relationship and are daring to love again.

Love

You have an enviable ability to connect with a partner on a deeper level than most people. Yet this intensity of feeling can scare those who are afraid of exploring their intimate feelings. However much you work at it, some partners will be unwilling or unable to do this. So at times you may have been hurt by someone who did not commit or love you with the same intensity. With this realization comes a deep sorrow for what you have shared, but also an acute understanding of what was always missing. When relationships end, it may appear to be the end of the world to you, and it is not uncommon to have negative or self-destructive thoughts. Avoid becoming depressed or even obsessed: move on.

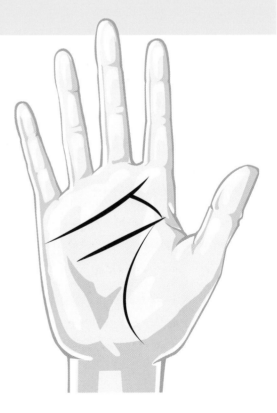

Space between heart and head lines

Any connection between the heart and head lines on the palm is interesting, as it has something to say about the link between your emotional needs and responses (heart) and your mental approach and attitudes (head). A branch linking these lines, for example, suggests that relationships will suffer unless there are efforts to develop clear lines of communication. The space between these lines reveals how you separate your emotional instincts from your intellectual reactions. Are you detached and objective, or are you intensely involved both emotionally and mentally, believing that everything affects you in a personal manner? As with the other profiles in this book, the following can be applied to the personality in general as well as to the areas of work and relationships.

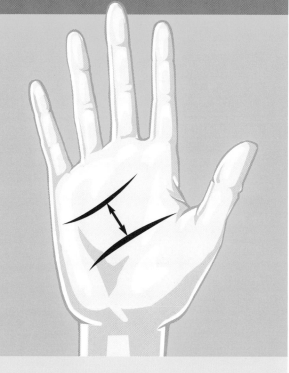

Of course, most people have an average space between these lines, and this suggests they are open to others but at the same time carrying a degree of prejudice and making decisions based upon their belief systems. Those with a Simian line (see page 68) will share many traits of those who possess a narrow space, but these characteristics will be more intensified and will dominate their character.

Wide space

- Broadminded and open
- Open to suggestion and influence
- Tolerant, liberal, 'live and let live'
- Generally unprejudiced, impartial
- Can lack focus or determination
- Can separate thoughts from feelings

Narrow space

- Quite narrow-minded, inhibited
- Closed-off, insular, unswayed
- Often has strong, non-PC views
- Influenced by moral/religious code
- Focused, controlled, dedicated
- Makes decisions with head and heart

Simian line

One of the most fascinating of all marks in the hand, the Simian line is a sign of intensity and personality extremes. Instead of having separate head and heart lines, there is one strong line that travels across the palm like a single railway track. If you have this in your hand, it suggests a one-track mind and tunnel vision – focused, intense and volatile in your personal style.

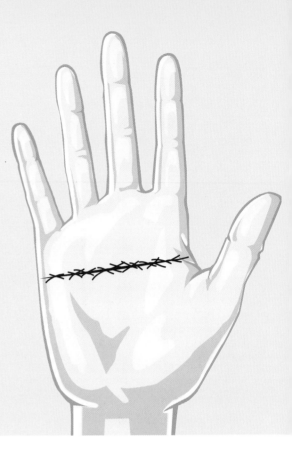

When found, it is usually present on one hand only. On the left hand, it relates to your personal relationships and feelings, and you may have a chaotic personal life. You may never seem to feel 'at peace' in private, always searching for a way to express yourself and never being able to relax and switch off. Partners may be driven away by your need to possess, control and dictate their every move. When found only on the right hand, it is expressed in your outer life and working environment, which can be equally chaotic unless you find a balanced rhythm or something on which to focus. When the line appears on both hands, the characteristics of a Simian line are greatly intensified.

Power and control

This line creates extremes in personality and little middle ground, so it is not at all uncommon to find that you function brilliantly in one area of your life but are completely unable to cope in another. One of the main themes of the Simian is control, and traditional palmists often associated this marking with violence, savage aggression and brutality. Some modern palmists see this line as heralding great success, particularly when found on the right hand or both hands. The Simian line dominates the hand to such an extent that you can either be a runaway success, capable of great originality, or a misguided, self-destructive missile.

With this line, elements essential for a balanced life are strong thumbs and long fingers (see pages 110–2), which add willpower, reasoning, attention to detail, diplomacy and a considered approach. With these features, you become a 'triple threat', able to win over others through charm and leadership ability. Supremely focused and disciplined, others will find you a force to be reckoned with.

At worst, the Simian line is the mark of a ruthless operator who is a law unto themselves and sees any attempt from others to change course or compromise their principles as a personal attack or betrayal. Leaders with Simian lines exert control over their subordinates, eliminate the opposition and prefer to run their organizations as dictatorships. They win admirers for their strength, charisma and leadership, but provoke opposition to their methods. There is usually a strong religious belief or a feeling of being on a mission, but in seeking control over their environment they must remember to maintain their integrity and to act in a way that is true to themselves.

Often the fate line will be less clearly marked or short. The Simian imbues its owner with a sense of personal destiny that overrides the responsibilities to others (fate line) – and this is more pronounced at the age at which the fate line fades or disappears. Nevertheless, it brings turbulence and disorganization into the life in some area unless a sense of inner peace is found.

All or nothing

Most people have separate heart and head lines, suggesting that they are able to separate their thoughts from their feelings. With a Simian line, however, it is almost impossible to separate emotional reactions from logic. Every thought is processed and felt intensely and every emotion analysed and coloured by reason; so, after a decision has been made, there is often a black or white approach to life and people. In love, there is an all-or-nothing approach that may be unattractive and off-putting. Rather than full-on passion, what is expressed is a need to sense absolutely everything in extreme form. Partners stand little chance when they are arguing with you and even less chance of changing your mind. Why should they bother? The Simian person is always right, after all! When other markings are present (such as the girdle of Venus – see page 88), there is often a need to express yourself through strong and extreme sexual situations.

Note that there may be extra strands to the Simian line (usually looking like a minor head or heart line), or the line itself may be a semi-Simian (where the head and heart lines collide). The palm shape and finger length will also say much about the motivations behind actions and how best to direct emotional and physical energies. About half of those with Down's Syndrome will have a Simian line, and often an abnormally short little finger.

Fate line

Where are you going in life? What drives you to succeed? What is your attitude to work and success? The fate line depicts your goals, your view of responsibility and commitment, how you interact with your environment, and the routines you have built up at work and in close relationships.

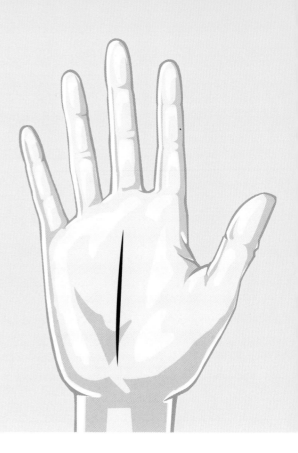

This is the most fascinating line of all, as its length, direction and course all provide clues as to your life path, aims and ambitions – as well as the extent to which you can shape your future. By understanding the fate line, you can unravel the dramas that take place in your life: the fascinating twists and turns of fate and the influential people you encounter along the way.

Your fate line can reveal whether you want the security of employed work or prefer freelance independence. Whether you are motivated by money or driven by high-flying ambitions, married to your work or desperate to break away from the family firm, taking a look at the fate line is likely to be of value.

Shape and form

The fate line can be long, short, in various strands, faint or strong. It usually begins near the base of the palm and travels up towards the middle finger. Sometimes it swings in from the outer edge of the palm or from within the life line. On some hands, it sprouts out of the life line or begins higher up on the hand. Some hands have two or more fate lines, and in some rare instances the line is missing completely.

Missing

When the fate line is absent, you refuse to 'play the game', preferring to live life on your own terms. You may be unable or unwilling to settle down into routine. At best, you may have an unconventional and adventurous approach to life, accompanied by a keen interest in various ideas and pursuits. At worst, it can indicate that you drift aimlessly, or are unable to commit personally (left hand) or professionally (right hand). When this line is absent, there may be a rejection of societal or parental expectations. The line may be missing on the hands of those who refuse to follow the religion or code set down by their parents.

When missing in part, this indicates a period when the career or life path is lacking in direction. When the fate line begins higher up in the hand, there may have been work and routine earlier but nothing that was personally satisfying or rewarding. When the line finally takes shape, this is an indication of you finding your niche or settling down into a steady, secure routine. Remember that the fate line can change course, fade out or strengthen over time as you respond to the changes you make to your inner and outer environments.

Duality

As with the other major lines, the fate line can be read on two levels. It discloses both your *psychological attitudes* to work and responsibilities and the *actual events* that shape your individual life path. (You can learn to time the latter on page 123.)

Success

The left hand's fate line is a major indicator of your personal attitude to success, rather than a sign of the success you may achieve in worldly terms (which is seen on the right hand). External recognition for your efforts will only register on the left hand if it is accompanied by personal fulfilment.

Job changes

Work moves are not necessarily shown on this line; instead, you will see changes in perspective and attitude towards your life path. Someone who moves job every few years, but keeps focused on an ultimate life plan, will most likely have one unbroken fate line. Another who moves regularly, but does so to search for direction, will have numerous, feathery fate lines. Someone who makes one major work change, however, which they find unsettling, will have a line that registers the change clearly.

Relating

For those whose primary objective is to be in a personal relationship, the fate line can represent your partner. Breaks or new lines will coincide with times when you end relationships or change partners.

Early development

The fate line makes its most significant developments between the ages of 7 and 14, when you develop independence and responsibility. It is not unusual to find broken strands of the fate line on the hands of young children. When found strongly marked on a young child, however, you can expect them to be responsible and serious.

Strong, unbroken fate line

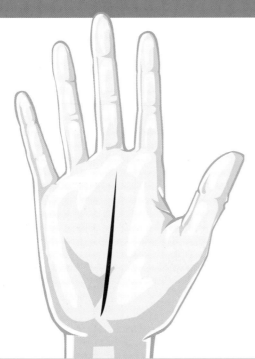

Work

You employ a conscientious, reliable and dedicated approach to your work. You pride yourself on reaching goals and love a job done well, whether it is housekeeping or running an insurance firm. You set clear, attainable goals and work productively towards them, often thinking about work in terms of a career rather than a job. Your ability to plan and envisage the long-term working climate is one of your strengths. Taking the occasional risk, though, will mean you won't stagnate or miss out on opportunities to stretch yourself and develop your talents.

Personality

Are you resistant to change? Probably. Set in your ways? Definitely. You like to do things your own way without interference, and you tackle life systematically. Your work ethic and sense of personal responsibility come from your family. You are tough on yourself: a control freak who sets high goals and imposes a strict code of conduct. If others accuse you of being dull, you know that common sense and reliability are traits that spell success. Risk-taking is for others; you prefer the steady climb, but could benefit from taking risks when opportunities to alter course come your way. When this line is particularly heavy, you believe in the adage that you may not get what you pay for, but you certainly pay for what you get.

Love

When you commit, it is rare that you change track, particularly in the game of love. In fact, love is rarely considered a game and you make commitments seriously and with sincerity. You will choose someone with a view to sharing your long-term future together. You want a life partner who is focused and hard-working, and not put off by temporary relationship difficulties. Watch out for the tendency to put work before love, though. Steady and committed, others may find you somewhat predictable and rather conservative in your day-to-day routine, but at least they will know what to expect.

Fine, faint or feathery fate line

Personality

If life often feels unsettled and upheavals seem to affect you more than most, it is not surprising that you sometimes fear the future and aim to find quick ways of feeling secure and settling down. Just be careful not to settle for second best. Perhaps you also need to admit that you don't care much for responsibility; so, rather than taking on duties and later running away from them, decide to have a more carefree existence with fewer obligations. You should, however, aim to make your daily life as full as possible – just avoid attracting unnecessary stress or hassle.

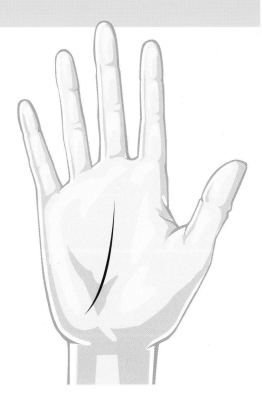

Love

Relationship issues dominate your daily life and this leaves little time to develop work that is satisfying and self-expressive. Don't abandon your creative needs or your independence if someone offers to take care of you. Until you find a healthy balance you may passively resist partnerships that demand long-term commitment. Drifting along until a situation becomes unbearable means you are taking part but certainly not playing a leading role in your own life. Living in the moment while developing relationships and pursuing fulfilling work (even if not in the long term) will be your finest dance.

Work

It is important to find work that makes use of your talents. You may prefer to opt out of the 'rat race' and settle for a stress-free, non-competitive life – although you sometimes put pressure on yourself to succeed on others' terms, which ultimately is a waste of everyone's time. In your own way, you will create a life path that is unique to you once you come to terms with the pace that you have set yourself. Your heart needs to be in your work before you fully commit, otherwise you may become lethargic and unreliable. Negative thinking or a fatalistic 'there's no point' stance is a waste of your abilities. Find a passion to be passionate about.

Double fate line

Personality

This interesting feature shows versatility and the capacity for hard work. Although it may seem that you juggle responsibilities endlessly, you do in fact take all aspects of your life seriously and display enormous focus and commitment. You should ensure you have time to relax, travel and recharge your batteries.

Love

At times, it seems as though you are forced to choose between work and romantic commitments, when in fact you have the discipline and energy to handle both successfully. Partners may be openly resentful of the time you give other aspects of your life. Rather than asking you to choose, they should be proud of your ability to attend to commitments in and outside the home. They also need to realize that, for you, a relationship is like a full-time job. You seek out good prospects, assess the long-term potential, and work consistently to get results.

Work

A double fate line could suggest two jobs, or at least imply that there are two avenues to which you dedicate your time. Often it is juggling a demanding career and a busy home life, but the result could be that you don't give yourself enough pampering or 'down time'. Women with this palm feature can seem like superwomen, able to spend all day working and then looking after children and partners when they get home. Sometimes with a double fate line, lovers are business partners working alongside you or are in some way involved in your professional life.

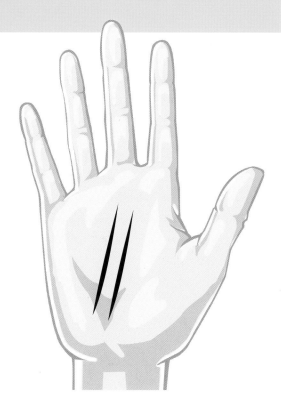

Numerous fate lines

Personality

You may have developed a reputation for indecision and an inability to see things through, but on the plus side you thrive on change and variety, and can be sparkling company. You have a low boredom threshold, and there is always something around the corner that promises to be more appealing. It is likely that your life will be filled with many interests; you are keen to try out various lifestyles or jobs before you settle down. Others shouldn't worry too much about you – when one door threatens to close, you will always have a foot into the next room.

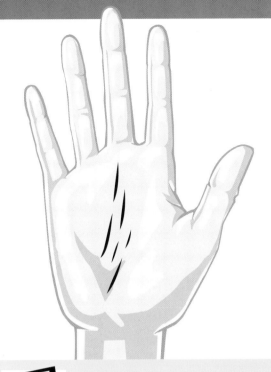

Love

There is a side to your nature that believes that relationships are transient, friends come and go and that there are few lasting ties. At worst, some of you can use others as stepping stones, leaving behind a trail of hurt, resentful people. You may enjoy a footloose time or a period of serial monogamy, but don't lose track of the important 'constants' in your life. Cultivate trust by being there for those who share your approach to life, and consider seeking a life of variety with one person in particular.

Work

You would do well in the media or any job in which versatility and flexibility are prerequisites. Rather than wanting to arrange a long-term career plan, go with the flow and try your hand at various work positions. Recognize that change is inevitable and that you need a varied life with few restrictions or commitments. See what suits you at any point in time and pour your energies into making it a success. Long-term plans with little room for adjustment are not for you. You prefer the two- or three-year work contracts, so project-related work appeals. If you insist on having a long-term plan, you will have to develop greater initiative, drive and staying power.

Fate line beginning halfway up life line

Personality

After feeling held back by family or responsible for their welfare, you have needed to develop a strong sense of who you are to succeed in your own right. You needed to break away from early conditions and restrictions and you are now more certain of your strengths as well as your limitations. Remember that fighting your way out of a situation has made you stronger and more self-determining. You are not a time-waster and your motto would be 'better late than never'.

Work

Don't worry if it has taken longer for you to find your true vocation. You haven't missed the boat, it is simply that your early years were good preparation for what you can now offer. Through these delays, you have learned lessons and are more realistic about what you can expect from others. Even if you stay with the family business, this later surge of working success will be on your own terms; perhaps you have even pioneered new working methods. You are a self-made person who can thank yourself for where you are today (especially if another fate line is present on the outer edge of the palm).

Love

Prospective partners may have to contend with your preconceptions about relationships as well as the unfair comparisons you sometimes make between them and your family or past lovers. Early unions may have suffered because you were tied to beliefs ingrained in childhood, or perhaps you had to contend with family opposition and interference. Did you commit too early because you felt it was 'the thing to do'? You will have your most successful relationships when you have drawn clear boundaries between you and your family, and know for certain what you want. If commitment comes a little later in life, it will be accompanied by a mature approach that benefits you both.

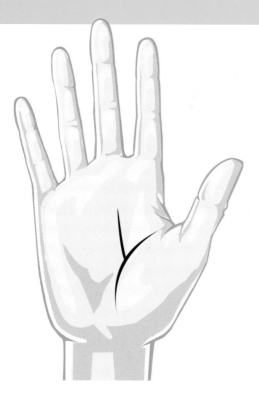

Fate line starting from base of life line

Work

You show strong dedication to your work and could follow a path in the service or nursing professions. When this formation occurs on both hands, you feel that your family demanded much from you as you grew up, and you carry a sense of obligation to them as you move into working life. Perhaps when you began working you were required to put money back into the family home or much of your spare time was taken up with family business. For some (especially when on the right hand), your need to support the family (or fear of making it on your own) saw you follow in the family's footsteps.

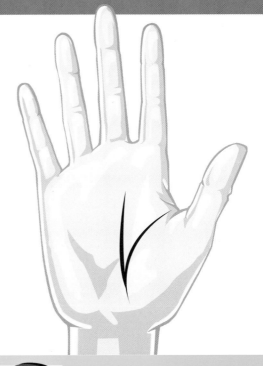

Love

It can be difficult for you to assert your independence in love, as family demands and expectations can get in the way. How can partners ever be as committed to you as you are to your family? By judging lovers in this way, you are doing them a disservice, since they may not have chosen to be so available and committed to their family. In fact, it is likely that you are attracted to their independence and refusal to let others rely too heavily on them. They will, at some stage, force you to assert your own independence and help you build a healthy distance from your family.

Personality

You are the type who carries the burdens of others on your own shoulders. You have taken the role of the dependable and rational person, and others are aware of this and can take advantage of you. They see you are co-dependent and some may use emotional blackmail to keep you at their beck and call. However much you display independence elsewhere, with family there appears to be a strong tie of dependence that you allow to remain, often to your cost. On the positive side, you cherish the family unit and as an adult seek security by wanting your own family. In some ways, this marking is similar to that shown on page 76, although with you there is less of a desire to break away from family responsibilities.

Love

Friends and lovers may come and go as your life and interests take you to new places. You seek variety and stimulation in love and friendship, and those unable to move with you will be left behind. Those willing to stay on board will find that you open up a world of new ideas and places, and widen their network of friends. Often partnerships arise out of friendship or shared interests, and sometimes love takes you to another country or requires that you learn a new language, religion or set of customs.

Work

This is one palm sign that reveals a born communicator, someone who wants to be directly involved in interacting with the public. Communication is the key as you strive to express yourself. Where other signs reinforce this, you look for a career that is directly dependent upon the public's needs and tastes (from running a pub to performing on stage). You are in tune with popular trends, and (especially when there are whorls on the fingertips – see page 104) have your finger firmly on the public pulse. Work opportunities are sporadic, so you must learn to pursue project or freelance work, as well as seek work openings by using your various social and professional contacts.

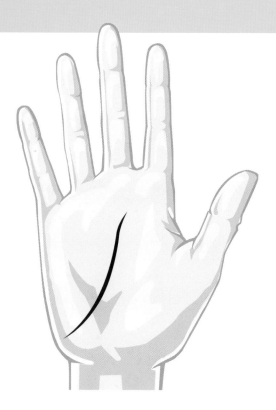

Personality

Faces, places and so many names to remember! You want your life to be full of eclectic experiences, encounters and escapades. Your personality is able to tap into what other people want. Sensing their concerns and anticipating their needs makes you able to put people at ease and adaptable enough to be an agreeable, pleasant person who is all things to all people (especially if you have loop fingerprint patterns – see page 102). Your innate friendliness stems from a need to please and from having felt an outsider at some stage.

Fate line to ring finger or index finger

The ending of the fate line gives a strong indication of where you end up and the type of success your hard work has brought you. The ending can also reveal the type of situation that got in the way (see page 80).

Most fate lines end on the Saturn mount (see page 108), a centimetre or two under the middle finger. This indicates that you have worked hard and followed the natural process of slowing down and moving into retirement. If various strands of fate line begin at this stage, this shows that you take up a number of interesting pursuits but may not have enough energy to carry them all out. You must be selective and avoid dispersing your energy. (With no lines in this area, you may struggle to find energy and motivation to do simple jobs.)

When the accompanying lines begin further down, it is known as the 'ladder of success', and has been seen on palms of self-made people who have reached the top through persistence and dedication. If the main fate line extends all the way up to the base of the middle finger, you resist retirement (or a long-held routine) and refuse to slow down.

In rare instances, the fate line swerves away from its natural ending so that it heads towards the index or ring finger.

Ending under ring finger

Your creative approach to work will ensure recognition and respect – sometimes more easily than you expected. You will have a good measure of fame, acclaim or applause. Most of all you seek work through which you can express and enjoy yourself. Check the hand shape, the head line, the dominant fingers and print type to see where this success occurs.

Ending under index finger

This is a highly auspicious sign. Your work, leadership ability and talent lead to a position of influence and power. With this feature, you should always maintain your integrity.

It is important to remember that highly successful people also have fate lines that end on their Saturn mount, but in these cases perhaps the effort more than matches the reward.

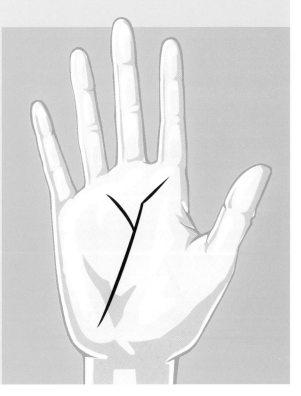

Fate line ends at head line or heart line

Traditionally, both of these were the signs of mistakes that ended a career. More often than not, however, an early end to the fate line is seen in the following ways:

Ending at the head line

When the fate line dies out at the head line (see diagram), it often coincides with a time when family and marriage take precedence over work. You may decide to give up your job at this time to get married and/or raise a family. Sometimes, if you have had little opportunity to explore your own needs and wants, it is a period when you give up personal commitments to pursue your own path. It all depends on your temperament and attitude to commitment and whether you have had balance in your life. Either way, this dramatic shift in your routine occurs around the age of 35. If, however, the head line is higher up in the hand, then the transition could occur a little later.

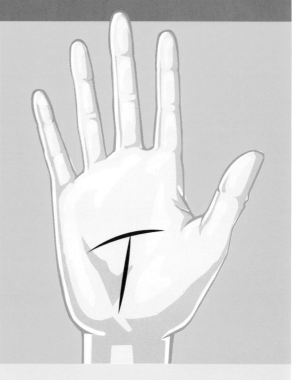

Sometimes the career does run out of steam and the later years are spent trying to launch a comeback. Some famous people with this sign enjoyed early success but disappeared from the limelight by their mid-30s. Perhaps (but this is less likely) their fortune has been made and they can live the life they have always wanted without stress or huge obligation. Most importantly, there has been a change in attitude (head line) to the previous everyday routine and schedule (fate line). Often, a new line appears higher up in the hand suggesting a new goal that acts as a motivation to return to work.

Ending at the heart line

This shows a natural end to one's job or career. Perhaps love, family or a healthy bank balance encourages you to retire early. Occasionally your health forces you to take it easy. This change in your life path occurs at approximately 56 years of age.

The fate line ends early, when the Apollo line begins

This is a marvellous sign for those of you who aim to accomplish your ambitions when you are still able to enjoy the fruits of your labours. For those who are less ambitious, it shows a time when you leave a set routine and move into work or early retirement that is personally satisfying and creative.

Branches rising from fate line

Check the fate line timing chart on page 123 to discover when the branch rises from the fate line.

Branch rising to index finger

You desire recognition, power and influence, and have the self-belief to attain these. You are more driven than most and motivated by the contest, the winning and the respect from your peers. Positions of leadership come your way, you are a political animal, and the cut and thrust of politics or management would suit your competitive nature. You have the opportunity to make a positive difference to your environment, so make sure you are driven by strong principles and morality rather than by political expediency.

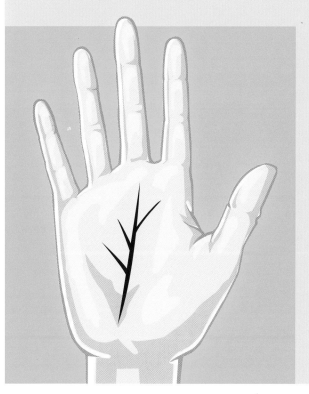

Branch rising to ring finger

This is an excellent indication that many of your dreams and ambitions will come true – but only when the necessary hard work (fate line) and preparation has been done. For you, success will occur when preparation meets opportunity. Your creative instinct is strong, and you would prefer a standing ovation to a position of responsibility. Being recognised for your talents is a prerequisite, and you will achieve some measure of fame and success in a creative field. Your head line (see pages 36–55) will say much about how you achieve the acclaim you crave, and your palm shape will indicate what motivates you. Even when in a business or teaching environment, you add creative flair and more than a little drama to your work.

Branch rising to little finger

This benevolent sign indicates wealth as a result of hard work and perseverance. It also suggests that you have worked hard to develop business acumen. Money and financial security are priorities, as they give you the freedom to determine your future and play the game your own way. Wealth can be yours if you take control of your own finances, but you may have needed to learn business from scratch if your head line is curved rather than straight (see page 39). You have learned to be a good deal-maker and tough negotiator, and you can charm others into submission with your persuasive tongue. A good income can be generated from writing, sales, promotions or acting as an agent.

Fork at beginning of line

Early on, you had a choice that you were unable to decide on, perhaps due to a lack of experience. When the lines united, you were able to move forward. If it looks to be more of a joining line, this would indicate an influential person coming into your life (see relationship lines on pages 93–5).

Fate line ends in a fork

When the fork occurs on the mount under the middle finger, this is a propitious sign showing success from diverse ventures. If the fate line ends earlier, for example between the head and heart lines, it is a sign that your energies and attention are split, and that you may not have enough incentive to continue pursuing a particular professional or personal path.

Gap

This indicates a break in routine or job. It can sometimes be a period of unemployment (although this is more common when the fate line becomes lighter) or when you lack focus and direction. It could, however, be a period when you take time off away from the rat race to 'find yourself'. Your routine or life path has ended and you must face a short period of adjustment.

Star on fate line

Luckily this is rare, and it points to a period when one crisis or shock follows another. Perhaps one specific incident has knocked you sideways, or you must attend to unwanted attention (this marking has been seen on the hand of a person who reluctantly became 'famous for 15 minutes').

Overlapping fate lines

This indicates a change in your path, but one that you have planned. As the lines overlap, you make the necessary adjustments and, although there may be difficulties, with luck you have the faith to continue and realize that you are going through an important transition.

Overlapping lines with a square

A good omen, ensuring that you will feel protected during a difficult life change by routine or security.

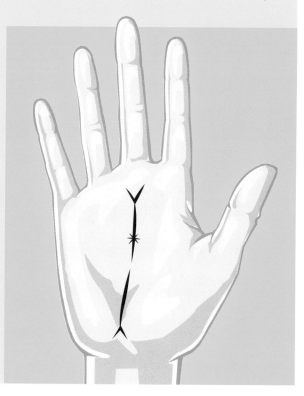

Dot

There is a temporary block or obstacle to overcome when there is a dot on the fate line, although it seems to overshadow everything at the time. Look to see whether the fate line improves above the dot in order to judge how this obstacle is likely to affect your immediate future.

Crossing lines

These fine lines can show some stress, nerves or worry, particularly if they are horizontal crossing lines. Otherwise, they are people who enter your life. Again, check what occurs higher up on the fate line to see the positive or negative influence of these people.

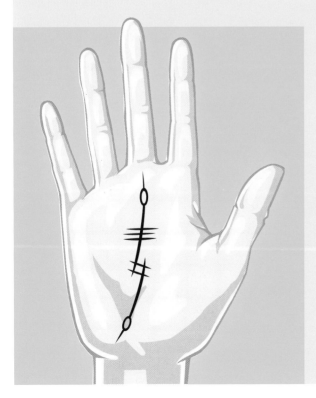

Island early on

This can show a phase during your teenage or early adult years during which you feel restricted by circumstances or family. There may be a strong feeling of loneliness or isolation and you feel trapped and unmotivated. Often there will be rising lines at the beginning of the life line (see page 34) to show that you are making efforts to break away.

An island in the fate line is also a warning not to get caught up with a bad crowd. Mixing with the wrong people may do your early adult life some harm. The challenge here is to break out on your own rather than follow the crowd.

Island later on

A rare feature that will mark a period when you may feel eager to change your life path. Perhaps family, relationships or children hold you back, or you find yourself in a job that offers few prospects. You may feel stuck, unmotivated, trapped and perhaps a little isolated too. The important thing to do during this phase is to look around for possible new avenues – or, if few are open, see this time as one of learning what you don't want in the future.

But there is one warning: choose the people with whom you mix with great care. This can be one sign (along with an island on the Apollo line) of a bad reputation or finding yourself unfairly judged.

All of the markings can be timed using the fate line timing chart on page 123.

Minor Lines and Special Markings

Most hands have a variety of other markings – special line formations that can indicate talents, additional characteristics and drives. Keep an eye on minor lines that form letters of the alphabet, such as A and E. It is often possible to find in your hands the first letters of the names of people or places that are significant in your life. The letter's position is particularly important when timing the hand, as this can show when the relevant person or place becomes part of your life.

Apollo line

The Apollo line, also known as the 'sun' line, has much to say about your sense of personal fulfilment when found on the left hand, and your attitude to success and creativity when found on the right. It is an artistic marking, so those of you who have it strongly marked, or of considerable length in the hand, will enjoy creative or artistic pursuits. It is not always found on the hands of the rich and famous, but rather on those who enjoy their lives and their work, whether they are well known or not. Sometimes a celebrity will have an Apollo line that begins higher up in the hand, after their first brush with fame. Its late emergence signifies that they found happiness and success on their own terms.

The question is – what makes you happy? Money and power? Fame and recognition? Children and a supportive relationship? The presence of an Apollo line reveals whether you are currently utilizing these skills and pursuing happiness in some form. (The head line, the hand shape and fingerprint patterns will show in which creative field you can excel and what type of self-expression fulfils you.) The Apollo line is often found amid many fine lines on water hands, and therefore should be afforded less significance. It is rare in its complete form on earth and fire hands, so keep this in mind, too. In most hands, it is only found above the heart line, and this suggests that your later years bring you a measure of happiness and personal contentment.

Rising alongside the fate line

It is rare to find an Apollo line that extends for most of the palm's length. It shows that early on you found work or a personal situation that gave you a sense of contentment and accomplishment. When other factors are present (such as a long ring finger and thumb), you may have what is diplomatically termed an 'artistic temperament'. This line also promises a life of travel, the chance to explore a personal philosophy or an appreciation of life by living it one day at a time.

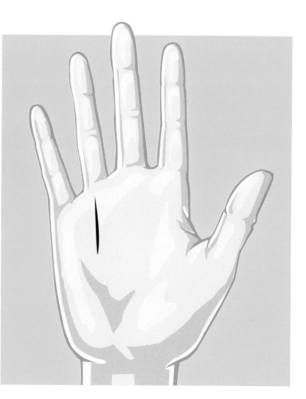

Rising from the mount of Luna

(a) Traditionally, this is a sign of success arising out of a strong imagination. Sensitive artists with water hands will sometimes have this marking pronounced. Involvement with the public is another possibility, although with most public figures the Apollo line is secondary – they usually have strong fate lines (see page 72), suggesting that discipline, hard work and a serious nature are prerequisites.

Sweeping in from the mount of upper Mars

(b) This is a sign that early success may have been taken for granted but later you fight for recognition in a field that is closer to your heart. It shows that you struggle for many years for success and respect from others, but that you must work autonomously. When success finally arrives, as it usually does with this marking, it is well earned and deserved. Careers in mind, body or spirit fields, or the 'unknown', are also indicated.

Rising from the fate line

(c) When found on the right hand, this suggests that a measure of fame or success is a direct result of your efforts and discipline.

Rising from the life line

(d) A rare sign, this indicates a life of fortunate twists and turns. Sometimes it is found rising from the early part of the life

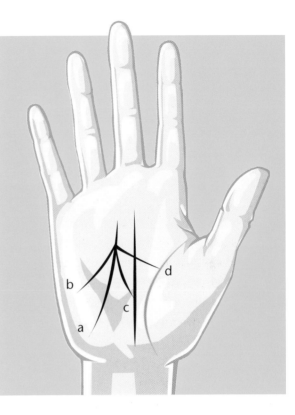

line. It has sometimes been seen on child stars who had very early exposure to fame and success.

When the Apollo line is absent, this shows that you are quite hard to please. You are always on the lookout for something or someone who will bring happiness into your life, rather than working out a way to make yourself happy and content. The good news about the Apollo line is that it will appear or develop on the hand when you are striving to enjoy life and be more creative.

Rings, bows and minor lines

Of all these interesting markings, only the Mars line can be timed (using the life line timing chart) with any accuracy. The rest show personality traits rather than events.

Ring of Solomon

(a) This marking of psychological insight indicates that you have good people skills and an ability to understand others' motivations. It is likely that you will use this gift of psychological understanding in your work, perhaps being drawn into the fields of psychology or self-development. Or maybe you are an amateur psychologist to friends or the office advice-giver, always ready to lend an ear and give an opinion. You are naturally geared towards delving beyond what others say and do – a psychological detective always looking for hidden meanings and clues as to underlying emotions. Simply put, you want to know what makes others tick but can sometimes scramble around looking for motives that are not there. At best, you offer words of wisdom and inspiration that others can relate to. These words may come to you in intuitive flashes.

Sometimes this line links up to the heart line, showing that you have a flair for understanding others' relationship dramas and sexual problems. You may also be drawn into advisory roles. When it touches the teacher's square, you can counsel, influence and mentor others. If there are also teaching or writing signs in the hand, there is a strong desire to write about or promote self-help disciplines. Very rarely, it touches the girdle of Venus (see below) and suggests that your understanding of others comes from intuitive hunches.

Teacher's square

(b) This marking suggests an ability to teach and inspire others. You look for work in which you are able to communicate information with clarity and wisdom.

Girdle of Venus

(c) This marking has suffered in reputation, with traditional palmists linking it to a lascivious, promiscuous nature. At its most profound, it can indicate the presence of a rare insight into human nature as well as intuitive awareness of the future. If you have this line (particularly unbroken), you have a rare opportunity to develop psychic skills and gifts of precognition, whether it is having hunches about people or being able to predict events. Your psychic antennae are so sensitive that you can sense atmospheres and feel positive and negative vibrations. This girdle can be used to great practical effect with music. Your immune system may be particularly fragile or one of the five senses could be highly attuned.

At worst, particularly when the allergy line (see page 91) is present, there may be a craving for excitement that lands you in hot water.

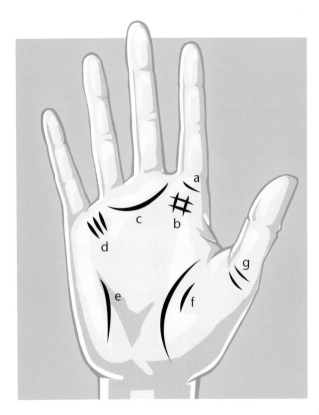

Bow of intuition

(e) This is often considered a sign of psychic ability, but it is more likely to be found on those who make decisions based on hunches.

Mars line

(f) Running a few centimetres inside the life line on the mount of Venus, this reveals a combative person who never gives up. You recuperate fast, being able to bounce back from difficulties that would floor most others. When the line is strong and long, you live for the battle but remember that this does not make you the easiest person to live with. When the Mars line is stronger than the life line, you may have built up an arsenal of anger and resentment about life. Find avenues to release these potentially self-destructive traits.

Family ring

(g) Two rings at the base of the thumb are said to show strong family ties. More interesting are the lines that run from the lower ring towards the life line. They can be timed using the timing chart (page 121) and show events that affect you deeply. When they stop at the life line or Mars line, they can indicate the death or illness of a loved one. If they travel beyond the life line and up towards one of the fingers, this indicates an event that changes your life – for example, if travelling towards the ring finger they may show the birth of a child or beginning of a profound relationship.

With both of these markings, you should steer clear of stimulants, drugs and other self-destructive habits. You should also be aware of a compulsion to 'shake things up' when relationships become stale. You may choose to risk a long-term relationship for the thrill of a one-night stand. You always seek new 'highs', and have a temperamental streak, testing the patience of those around you.

Medical stigmata

(d) With or without a bar connecting the trio of lines at the bottom, this is found on those who often work in the caring professions.

Lines cutting across life line

If you have any of the following markings on your hand, these should be assessed carefully. They all indicate *possible* health difficulties, but the appearance of these lines on your hand does not indicate they are 'destined' to happen, nor do they need to be of the exact nature described below. It is also important to see whether the life line continues unchanged after the cutting line or whether it has been affected by this interruption (by becoming either stronger or weaker). This will reveal your reaction to the event.

Line from the direction of the middle finger

To be authentic, this line must actually cut the life line, otherwise it could very well be a branch (see page 34) – examine this carefully first. It can sometimes be the sign of a physical accident, often connected to a reckless activity. At other times, it is an unexpected illness that requires attention and is a shock to the system. If the life line strengthens afterwards, it shows that full health has been regained, or a desire to live life to the full is now a motivating factor. If the life line weakens or breaks into a chain of small islands, it may take some time to recover.

If there is a square formed by a few horizontal lines (see page 83), then there is a sense of you feeling safe through this difficult period of hardship when life seems to impose various limitations. When this cutting line appears very early on in the life line, it can indicate that you had a shocking experience when young. Perhaps there was an accident or the sudden death of a loved one.

Line from inside the life line

This line tends to run for about 2.5cm (1 in) over the mount of Venus, the padded base of the thumb. It reveals some difficulty connected to the family. Sometimes it is a parent's death or another type of unsettling incident that brings upset. Again, check how the life line develops after this interruption.

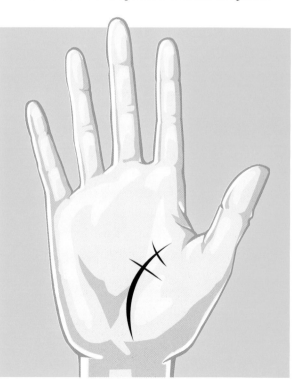

For lines originating from inside the life line heading towards the heart line, see relationship lines on pages 93–5.

Health line (lines from the direction of the little finger)

Sometimes these lines descend into the centre of the palm without reaching the life line, and suggest that you have a nervous disposition. You may be someone who is very aware of your daily health and energy levels (its colour will give a clue to the state of the general nervous system – a black line is connected to worry and stress). You are also

someone who is a bit of an emotional seesaw, being 'up' one minute with positive enthusiasm and 'down' the next with dread and pessimism. When these lines cut the life line, it may be a time when your health suffers, often due to nerves or a nervous habit such as smoking.

Allergy line

This line usually appears from the outside edge of the palm and heads towards the life line. It is a warning of sensitivity or addiction to chemicals, alcohol and foods (particularly chocolate). If the girdle of Venus is also present (see page 88), it is important not to get involved in the recreational use of drugs or heavy drinking and smoking, as these are the palm signs of an addictive personality. Heavy smokers with this line suffer more than those who don't have the allergy line on their hands. Many who have this line will have allergies (such as an allergic reaction to smoking) and have tried some herbal remedy to alleviate the effects.

This line doubles up as the matriarch line, which indicates the presence in your life of a dominating and sometimes interfering mother-figure. With this line, you are closely attuned to her and her opinion holds much sway over your decisions. Sometimes men with this line move from one matriarch to another through marriage.

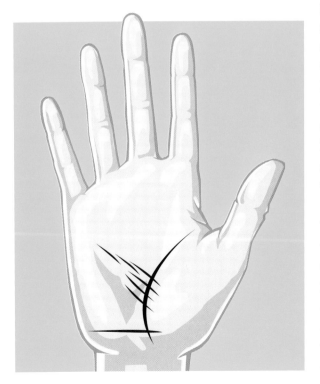

Travel lines and relationship lines

Horizontal lines on the outer edge of the palm

These interesting lines reveal a restless spirit as well as important travels in the first part of your life. These lines should be timed using the fate line timing chart on page 123. Be careful not to confuse these with the allergy line (see page 91). Interestingly, these lines are relative to your experiences. For example, those who cross the Atlantic each week will not have these travels indicated in their hands; but the country person who travels to a big city for a week will have this line if the journey has made a lasting impression. Just as gypsy relationship lines (page 93) show up when the other person is deemed important in your life, these travel lines will only reveal influential journeys and trips.

Branches off the life line

These show a strong desire to travel. These branches can be timed using the life line timing chart (see page 121) and will pinpoint times when you make important travels and changes of residence. Interestingly, the more you have, the more you search for stability and permanence in your life. Often these lines will be found at least halfway down the life line, suggesting travels or moves abroad in later years. The strongest lines will show the most important trips away, and if the line is stronger than the life line you may move area or country at this time and not return.

Line from inside the life line heading towards the heart line

This is an indication of a true meeting of minds. Someone comes into your life at a time, perhaps after a sheltered upbringing, when you are willing to make a major commitment. When a similar line follows further down the life line but is, in fact, broken, this may be a time when the relationship faces a make-or-break period, often because of an emotional upheaval following some kind of breakdown in communication.

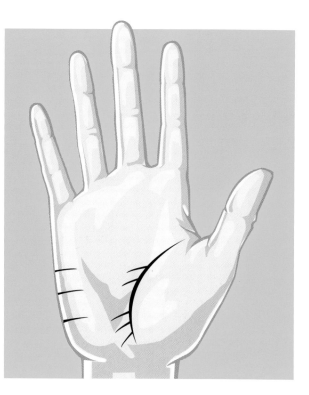

Line joining the fate line

This influence line can show anyone who joins your path (fate line) and influences your journey. To confirm whether it is a romantic influence, use the life line timing chart (page 121) to see whether a relationship line comes in at the same time across the life line.

When a line joins the fate line from the direction of the thumb, it shows a personal commitment (or influence from a family member) that shapes your personal (left hand) or professional (right hand) life. When

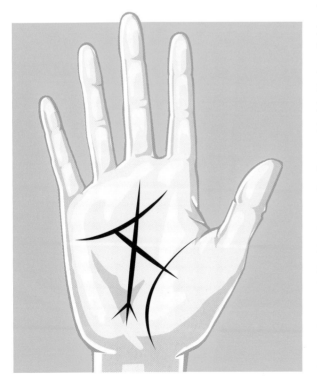

it sweeps in from the outer edge of the hand, expect someone to enter from your sphere of work. With arranged marriages, there is a belief that love matches are shown as influence lines from the outer edge, while strictly arranged unions come from the direction of the family area (the thumb).

Gypsy lines

These lines are, according to old palmistry books, supposed to represent marriages, although nowadays they symbolize all romantic relationships. These are not the most reliable of lines, particularly where timing is concerned because they occur in a place on the hand (below the little finger) that is linked to the mind. So some of the gypsy lines may be just that – simply in your mind! (People with these lines may not have had actual physical relationships but instead live a fantasy life imagining they have. In such cases, the head line will often be deeply curved – see page 40 – or have a branch that descends deep into the mount of Luna.)

Sometimes the lines may appear longer and deeper than would be expected because the relevant people (as represented by the lines) may have stayed intensely in your mind for a long time after each relationship ended. The depth and length of the lines are relative to the depth of your feelings about the people – and the length of time they affect you – rather than the actual length of the relationship.

Gypsy lines can appear to be contradictory and there are a number of points to remember when you read them.

Reading the gypsy lines

1 To time the gypsy lines, divide the section from your heart line to the base of the little finger into three. Each section should cover approximately 25 years. The lowest section will deal with early relationships that moulded your sexuality and love desires and needs. The middle section is from the mid- to late 20s to mid-life, during which one or two significant lines show up even if you have had many. Finally, the last third will trace those possible commitments you could have into your 50s (see 3 and 4, below).

2 Not all your romantic relationships will necessarily show up – only the ones that have really affected you. This is why you often have more lines in the early (lowest) section because brief romances that lasted for only a few months in your teenage years may have had more lasting impact than those in your late 20s to 40s (middle section).

3 They show possible commitments, chances that are available (that is, possibilities 'in your mind') but of course you don't have to act on them or end existing relationships.

4 Sometimes lines appear twice because your partner has re-entered your life or you have taken up a new path with them. Either way, it feels like a new way of relating or a chance to explore other avenues together.

5 The gypsy lines on your left hand will be more significant when noting your deep love commitments.

6 Often the strongest or longest line is the top one. This line's course and ending may reveal insights into your major life relationship (appearing further down).

GYPSY LINE MARKINGS

Please remember that these markings are not as reliable as they once were, perhaps because life and relationships are more complicated nowadays. Keep the previous points in mind. Don't forget, too, that relationship choices are certainly 'in your hands' – *your* temperament and approach directs *your* life. Take time to look back to the sections on the head and heart lines, as these will tell you a great deal about your attitudes to love and one-to-one communication.

a	**Long, deep line**	An important, intense relationship tie that has a lasting impact and can overshadow other parts of your life
b	**Short, deep line**	A short-lived, intense union
c	**The line is weak (at any stage)**	This suggests that you are passing time with someone or going through the motions, having disconnected or become involved elsewhere
d	**One line only, placed high up**	There may be other reasons why you are involved (such as money or companionship) or perhaps you have settled for someone reliable
e	**Begins with a fork**	Possibly two separate starts to the union
f	**Ends with a fork**	Going your separate ways (whether you divorce or not)
g	**Sloping downwards or a cross near or on the line**	Possibly outliving the partner
h	**A vertical line cuts through it**	The relationship survives a disruptive experience
i	**A vertical line ends the line**	A sudden (sometimes liberating) end to the union

Stars, crosses and triangles

A star on any part of the hand suggests an unexpected event. It can be a shock that acts as a jolt to the system. Even when in a favourable position (such as under the ring finger), it can indicate a bittersweet reaction to some unexpected success. Perhaps a sudden windfall or explosion of public interest in your life or work can seem 'too little, too late' or bring with it some intrusion that requires much adjustment.

A cross (except under the index finger) usually indicates an obstacle or some impediment to your path. At these times (see timing the hand, page 120, to pinpoint the age), you must look after your body, find ways to overcome difficulties and avoid taking physical risks.

Triangles are generally considered very lucky (particularly when formed independently rather than as a result of major line crossings). They bring a sense of fulfilment to the area in which they are found.

Many books present a range of odd markings, most of which you will never see (or see often enough to test your discoveries). Here are the markings that have been well researched and found to be consistent in their interpretation. The signs should be clear and well formed to qualify.

Under index finger

Star You are either destined for great things yourself (other lines should have corresponding signs) or your life is enhanced by contact with the famous or influential.

Cross This is the sign of a lasting or beneficial union, a meeting of minds and an acceptance of having found your 'soul mate'.

Triangle Early success is a result of fortunate contacts, lucky breaks or backing from family or other supporters. There is an aura of benevolence or philanthropy.

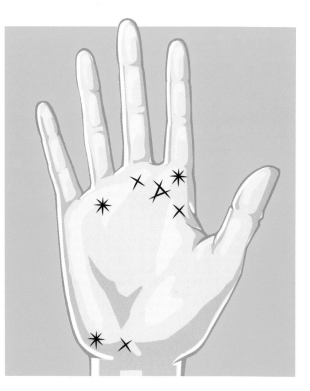

Under middle finger

Cross There may be a difficult period of adjustment while moving into retirement. You must learn to relax and find a new role that inspires and motivates you.

Under ring finger

Star This often suggests a financial windfall or a burst of publicity. You have charisma but may encounter delays before achieving success. Nevertheless, acclaim will be on your own terms. Rather than feel bitter about the long wait, accept that these experiences were necessary to appreciate your own success.

At the base of the palm

Star A sudden family event changed your early life (usually during the teenage years or early 20s) and may have set you on a new path. This also shows creative flair and a genius for tapping into what the public will like. With a successful head line, you can market innovative ideas and profit from future trends.

Cross An early obstacle or hardship delayed your development.

On the life line

Star An unsteady time during which you should monitor your health.

On the head line

Star Creative flair and talent are indicated. Occasionally, this can show a susceptibility to high blood pressure.

On the fate line

Star A sudden event prompts a change of life direction.

On the Apollo line

Star You exude star quality and charisma, crave fame and adoration, and believe you are destined for a special life. You have the potential to accomplish much but may find success from an area you didn't anticipate.

4

Hand Topography

This section explores the fingerprint patterns and the many areas of the hand. First there's a comprehensive look at the unique, permanent patterns found on each of the fingertips. Then follows a consideration of the mounts – those fleshy, padded areas of the hand. Finally, the ten digits are explained – the individual meanings of the fingers and thumbs, as well as the importance of their relative lengths and positions.

Fingerprints

Scientists don't know why the skin forms the unique weaving patterns identified as fingerprints, but palmists understand how important these distinctive ridges are in revealing character traits. These patterns are not just on the fingertips but all over the hand. Palmist Lori Reid called them the 'visible signature of the DNA', and indeed they show the basic personality traits inherited from your parents. These markings are the foundations of your personality, but can be overshadowed by other factors (such as the shape of the head line or of the hand), so take the profiles in this section as revealing the basics of your temperament. The scientific term for the study of skin (papillary) ridges is 'dermatoglyphics'.

Fingertip facts

1 Fingerprint patterns are formed in the womb. Research has found that they appear on the hands by the fifth month of pregnancy.

2 Fingerprints grow larger (and the spaces between the ridges widen) as your fingers grow, but they do not change their actual patterns.

3 The patterns are permanent. Once injuries to the fingertips have healed, the exact same prints resurface on the new skin tissue.

4 No two fingerprints have ever been found that are exactly alike. Even twins who are identical in every other way have different prints.

5 In March 2001, scientific research led by Dr Henry Kahn noted a correlation between fingerprint ridges and the likelihood of coronary heart disease, diabetes and short life expectancy. Scientists believe that large differences between the number of ridges on the ring and little fingertips on the right hand provide clues to later body shapes, which in turn makes you susceptible to particular diseases. They found that most people have roughly six more ridges on the ring finger than on the little finger. When the difference was around 20, the subjects tested tended to have apple-shaped bodies (an upper-body tissue distribution, as seen in those with typical 'beer bellies') as opposed to pear-shaped ones. If this research is developed it could provide an early clue to later body shape and possible health problems and illnesses. People in the affected group could then be aware of this and take greater care with their diet and lifestyle.

6 Research instigated in 1996 over a two-year period made early claims that gay men have a similar ridge count on their thumb prints to women, who in turn have a lower number than heterosexual men. If this turns out to be scientifically reliable and if decisions were made as a result of these observations, it would have significant repercussions on the nature-nurture debate on sexuality as well as being both damaging and intrusive to the gay community.

7 Prints may be infallible, but fingerprint experts do sometimes make mistakes. In the UK, on occasion, innocent people whose fingerprints were held on databases were being charged with crimes in which they played no part. After a series of wrong convictions due to mismatched fingerprints at the scenes of crimes, more rigorous procedures (including an unlimited number of 'points of agreement') were introduced in

2001 to wipe out misidentifications caused by time restrictions, peer pressure and sheer incompetence. Before that time, only 16 points needed to be matched in order to reach a positive identification, and then this could be presented in court as hard evidence. (This 16-point standard was still significantly higher than the standard in most other countries.)

Finding your dominant print

Most people have loops or loop-arch patterns. The most important digits to examine are the left and right index fingerprints as well as the prints on both thumbs. (At the end of this section, there is a 'mix and match' page where you can find the traits of each print according to the finger on which they are found.) The pattern that appears most on these four fingertips is the dominant one (for traits, see the following pages). On average, loops appear on 65 per cent of all fingertips, arches on 5–6 per cent and whorls on 30 per cent, but these statistics vary across different races.

So, are you the owner of provocative, individualistic whorls? Or are you a fluid, easy-going loop type? Or perhaps you are more of a hands-on, practical arch person? Browse through the following pages to find out.

Loop

Work

Your general adaptability is your greatest asset in your professional life, as you can move jobs, take on different tasks and deal with new people without fear of change or major adjustment. Just make sure you have easy access to that much-used telephone. Working with the public, selling, conversing and making others feel comfortable is second nature to you. Job variety, the possibility of moving up the career ladder or switching departments appeals to you, as does office gossip – you are endlessly curious about matters that concern you, and often those that don't.

Love

It is important for you to be seen as flexible and nonchalant, although other palm factors (such as the heart line) play a more important role here. This is the sign of someone who can flirt, laugh and converse with most people. You will have a lot of platonic relationships, as many people think they know you well and are a good friend of yours. When this print type is the most dominant, love partners may find you rather indecisive and may question your depth of feeling and commitment to the union. Romantically, you seem to want to 'have your cake and eat it'. You want your options to remain open and believe that fidelity should be a choice rather than a necessity.

Personality

You are generally an easy-going and versatile person who seeks variety in your work, love life and daily schedule. Although this fingerprint pattern is common and can be overridden by other factors in the hand, there is a general need to get on with people and be seen as a 'people person' who can chat with anyone about anything. This type is certainly not the specialist and the expression 'Jack of all trades' may ring true. Nevertheless you like to see your life as a big drama, with you taking on the pivotal role of a lifetime.

Arch

Personality

You like to be considered a 'salt-of-the-earth' type, and indeed you are reliable, practical and unpretentious. Your self-esteem may, however, need to be developed but avoid putting on a tough 'I can cope' exterior. Others find you approachable and down to earth, but because you are often so available to lend a hand, it is easy for you to get stressed when everyone needs your advice and help to solve their problems. You are the proverbial shoulder to cry on and feel the weight of the world on your shoulders, but don't forget to express your emotions. Make sure you have close friends with whom you can share your worries, too.

Work

No one is more prepared to put in a full day's work than you. Being focused and working towards tangible results is a priority when it comes to applying yourself and tackling jobs. Although you make your contribution, you have sometimes felt overlooked, 'hard done by' or treated like the underdog. This gives you extra incentive to fight for the needs of others. Even if you have chosen an office job, you won't be happy unless you can turn your hand to skilled manual work (from ceramics or sculpture to mechanics and engineering). Outdoor pursuits such as gardening would be great therapy away from the stress of office life.

Love

Arch prints reveal you to be extremely earthy and sensual. Your affinity to nature means that sexually you should explore the great outdoors with your partner. Your steadfast, tenacious nature makes you reliable in love. It takes more time than most to truly trust someone before you reveal your innermost feelings and expose your insecurities. For you, relationships must come with commitment. It is not easy for you to give up on a relationship even if it has run its course. Yet perhaps your loyalty has something to do with an innate need for routine and constancy ... and a refusal to admit defeat?

Whorl

Work

One difficulty of being 'different' or ahead of your time is that others who are less creative don't quite know how to relate to you on a professional level. With many whorls, you have a distinctive talent, gift or creative flair. It may be an ability to know today what will be popular tomorrow, or perhaps your talent is being able to think laterally. Whatever it may be, sooner or later it will emerge. You may choose to work for yourself, or be freelance, because you are essentially a 'control freak'. You approach your work with enviable focus and single-mindedness. If you need the cooperation of others at work, then concentrate on getting along with them too.

Love

Woe betide a partner who wants to argue with you – or, worse still, the one who thinks they can win. What's the point? You are always right. Partners won't be able to predict your moods, either – sometimes you will be keen to get close and personal, but on other occasions you will try every trick to keep them distant. Others need to learn that they can't predict your behaviour and must expect extreme mood swings. Essentially you are a loner who needs space, so look for a partner with this pattern too. Perhaps you can live next door and visit each other occasionally!

Personality

Stubborn and self-obsessed? Contradictory and rebellious? Others may assign these labels to your behaviour, but you consider yourself to be someone with a strong character who firmly believes in what you want, and refuses to compromise your principles. You stand out from the crowd, so, rather than thinking you are the black sheep, revel in your individuality. It is vital that you express your uniqueness, even if your stance provokes opposition (which it invariably does) – otherwise you could build up tension and resentment. The whorl is the sign of the free spirit and the maverick – friends and family may come and go, but you will need to come to terms with your own special reason for being here.

Other patterns

Loop arch

An often-seen alternative to the plain loop formation, the loop arch (where a loop 'intrudes' upon an arch pattern) enables you to turn your hands to anything. You question life and love, so it often takes time for you to settle down into a comfortable work routine or a committed relationship. You should avoid personal or professional commitments until you have spent time exploring your restless and endlessly curious spirit. If not, others experience you as changeable, inconstant and fickle. You have an ability to adapt to changes and new surroundings. At some stage, however, your work and loved ones will call on you to make long-term commitments.

Tented arch

This print (usually found on the index finger only) is an arch formation with a small, vertical 'tent pole' in the centre. With this print, you often find your niche as a fundraiser, teacher, motivator or general all-round do-gooder. You feel compelled to help or advise others, and may get involved fighting for the underdog or against some injustice. Your enthusiasm can be quite contagious, but you must avoid being more enthusiastic for others than they are for themselves. Professionally, you get fired up over new ideas, but need to practise 'going the distance', as interest can wane as soon as a more exciting idea appears on the horizon.

Composite

Which way, when and with whom? Those of you with this print constantly ask yourself these questions, as you grapple with life's choices and the inevitable forks you see on the road ahead. At best, you make an excellent strategist, counsellor or mediator, but it is a different story when you must make decisions that affect you. Some of you seem in a state of constant uncertainty as you endlessly weigh up the pros and cons. Whether you are buying a new jacket or contemplating moving home, it is all done with the same look of consternation (heaven help you if you have also got a long or feathery head line – see page 42). Trusting your gut instincts will help this agonizing process, as will making decisions by and for yourself. Perhaps the difficulty here is asserting your own needs when you know the effect your choices can have on loved ones. There is one saving grace here: when a decision is made, it is usually a good, fair and responsible one.

Peacock's eye

A rare print, the peacock's eye is a sign of protection (or at least a belief that you are being protected). Whether it is from a loved one in spirit or a profound trust in providence, you feel looked after and looked out for by an 'angel'. Often this print is found on people who have faced physical danger but have avoided being hurt.

Fingerprint mix and match

Here is a selection of interpretations of prints on various fingers. Loops are not included (except the radial loop – see below), as they are generally the most common and their meaning has been described on page 102. On any finger, the loop will display an easy-going approach in the area that finger 'rules', and will reveal a good team player as long as there is variety and flexibility. Remember that there will be some differences if the prints appear on the left (private) hand rather than the right (public).

Thumb

The thumb print describes your temperament as well as the way you put your ideas into action. It also shows how you approach tasks, address problems and how you come up with solutions.

Arch A practical, hard-working approach to tasks; you put in a full day's work and are results-driven; stress-prone; a loner.

Whorl Always finding innovative solutions to problems; forceful, single-minded and idiosyncratic; you stubbornly refuse to conform or be told what to do.

Composite A 'soul in torment' perpetually torn between two choices; sitting on the fence and weighing up pros and cons; always seeking advice or reassurance.

Index finger

The index fingerprint also describes your basic temperament, but shows how you label yourself, perceive the world and assert your true personality.

Radial loop (This is when the loop sweeps in from the thumb and heads towards the centre of the hand before sweeping out again; usually only found on the index finger.) A seeker of life's mysteries; you forge your own path and wish to be seen as a specialist and not 'one of the herd'.

Arch You see yourself as a 'salt-of-the-earth' type; life requires hard work and application to get results; 'you only get out what you put in'; for you, the good life is made up of companionship, robust health, some creature comforts and work that gives you a sense of accomplishment and satisfaction.

Whorl A gifted, intensely 'original' personality, able to perceive the world differently; eventually you accept (without apology) that you are different and can make a unique contribution; insightful, you can help others to expand their horizons and express their individuality.

Tented arch The born detective and the agitator fighting against injustice; an eternal student of life; to you, the world is full of mysteries and your job is to help inspire others to be free and 'aware'; a good samaritan and nurse.

Composite Unsure of who you really are or what you want to be; you sometimes feel pressurized by others to make up your mind; you are a clever analyst able to help others contemplate an alternative path, but have difficulty helping yourself.

Middle finger

The print on the middle finger reveals your attitudes toward routine and responsibilities.

Arch It is essential to have outdoor work or to work creatively with your hands; routine, structure and order are essential in your daily life.

Whorl You cannot stay in a run-of-the-mill routine or job with set hours; it is important to have work that involves challenge and acting on instinct; you will fight the system or go freelance.

Composite You are still in the process of deciding on a calling in life – but do you really need one? You are either an eternal student or someone who sleepwalks through a mundane job while dreaming of a better life.

Ring finger

The ring fingerprint will reveal any innate creative or dramatic flair.

Arch A particular talent to create forms or structures, such as a work of art; creative with your hands.

Whorl A 'drama queen' who needs an audience; a noted talent for acting, art or design (or simply drawing attention to yourself); a key indication of some form of special talent.

Little finger

The print found on the little finger gives a clue as to your method of communication, as well as your attitudes to intimacy and sex.

Arch A shy, honest and unpretentious attitude to sex and to self-expression; you need to learn to openly express all your feelings and worries.

Whorl An unusual manner of expression; adventurous in bed, willing to push back sexual boundaries; often provocative and sometimes contrary.

Composite Sexual ambiguity or indecision in relationships; a talent for mediation (particularly when counselling couples).

Mounts

Traditionally, palmists gave much importance to the mounts of the palm – the fleshy areas found under the fingers and around the edge of the palm. Each mount was assessed according to how fleshy, flat or displaced it was. Many palmists believed these were strong indicators of personality and drives, and thus the person with a dominant Jupiter mount (under the index finger) was labelled Jupiterian and ascribed appropriate personality traits. In modern palmistry, it is not felt that these mounts give much indication as to temperament or motivation. Only three mounts reveal traits with any consistency: the mounts of Luna, lower Mars and Venus.

What is important, however, is when a major line commences on a mount (such as the head line beginning on the Jupiter mount – see page 44). The line in question will take on the quality of this mount. When a line ends on a particular mount (such as the fate line swerving from its natural path and ending on the mount of Apollo – see page 79) it promises the owner the qualities associated with that mount. In addition, signs (such as stars, triangles or crosses) on any of the mounts are more influential than the shape and size of the mount itself. So it is important to understand the general meanings of these mounts to interpret signs and lines found on them.

Mount of Jupiter
Lines ending or beginning on this mount confer authority, ambition, power, confidence or idealism.

Mount of Saturn
The fate line usually ends on this mount, indicating a life of average responsibility. Usually, the only other line to end here is the heart line, and this suggests a self-protective character able to cut off from emotional involvement (see pages 60 and 62).

Mount of Apollo
Lines ending here suggest success, inner contentment and an artistic life path.

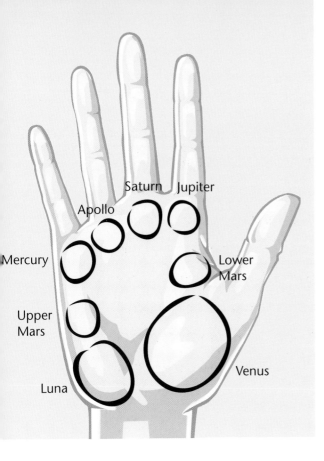

Mount of upper Mars

Situated below the heart line and above the mount of Luna, this mount can see the start of the fate or Apollo lines (see page 87), implying a late success after much struggle. Or it can be home to the end of the head line, suggesting stubborn, sometimes inflexible points of view.

Mount of Venus

It is rare that major lines begin or end on this mount, but if they do it suggests a strong 'influence' (i.e. interference!) from the family, and co-dependency that extends into adulthood. The mount puffs up when in the first blissful stage of romance. If fleshy (or large – protruding into the palm under the middle finger), you are warm and generous with your time and affection, and expect the same in return. A strong appetite for life and its pleasures is indicated. When it is flat, you need to develop more warmth yourself rather than expect others to provide it all.

Mount of Luna

This area rules the public as well as lunar (moon-based) themes: the imagination, the past, intuition, the unconscious instincts and subconscious impressions. It is also said to rule the sea and long voyages. It is the area in which travel lines are found. Lines beginning on this mount point to creative pursuits, and lines ending here (usually only the head line) indicate a heightened sensitivity and susceptibility.

Mount of Mercury

The health line (see page 91) usually begins here, and suggests an everyday awareness of your physical health. Lines that end on this mount point to persuasiveness and sharp business skills as well as a strong desire to have financial security and power.

Mount of lower Mars

Lines that commence here bestow a fighting spirit, irritability and pugnacious manner. If this mount is fleshy, displays of physical courage are expected. Here is someone who will fight (verbally or physically) with much ferocity if challenged.

Digits

The fingers, or digits, represent the tools you use to express your ideas and character. If the head line reveals how you use your brain and how you develop ideas, then the fingers show how you venture forth with these ideas and get your point across. Ideally, the finger length should match the length of the head line. Put simply, long fingers go well with a long head line, and short fingers with a short head line. When these do not correspond, however, there can be quick thinking (short head line) but a drawn-out mode of application (long fingers), or well-thought-out ideas (long head line) expressed without grace or patience (short fingers).

Most people have index and ring fingers of roughly the same length, showing the potential for healthy balance in love, work and health. When one digit is significantly longer than expected, it suggests that the traits associated with that finger dominate the life. Over the next few pages, you will discover the personality traits present when one digit is noticeably longer or shorter than the others.

Long or short fingers?

To determine how long the fingers are (in relation to the palm), you must look at the back of the hand – measuring the fingers from the knuckles up to the tip of the middle finger. The palm is then measured from the base of the middle finger down to the top rascette (the line that separates the hand from the forearm). If the fingers are of equal or greater length to the palm, they are considered long.

According to the four palm shapes (see page 16), long fingers are found on air and water hands, while short fingers belong to the fire and earth types.

Long fingers are found on critics and perfectionists who value order, detail, planning and hygiene above all else. They are good at analysing and processing

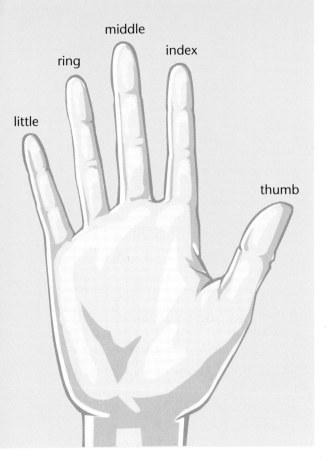

middle

ring

index

little

thumb

whole of a situation, rather than its parts. However much thought or planning has gone into a project (the length of the head line will show this), implementing these plans can be more than a little slapdash. Because they usually act on a gut instinct, they can take chances and surprise people by coming up with the goods at the 11th hour.

Current positions

At the end of each finger analysis that follows, there is a tried and tested method of determining personality traits that are *currently* being expressed. Shake your hands and lay them on a desk or solid surface. You will notice that some fingers lie naturally close to each other, while some stick out from the rest. It is rare to have all the fingers with equal distances between them. The relative positions of the fingers provide fascinating insights into your current psychological state. Don't forget to check whether these traits are displayed in your personal (left hand) or professional life (right hand).

information (particularly if the joints are bony), but in relationships they may be preoccupied with finding fault and criticizing their partners into submission. They use information tactically and diplomatically, and make excellent strategists and worthy opponents who have read the small print carefully.

Short fingers are found on those who have a somewhat childlike or basic approach to dealing with matters. Unless the fingers joints are bony (knotted), they don't want to spend time analysing details or putting the pieces together; they just want to get on with it and see the end result. They view the

When all fingers are held closely together, you are conformist, inhibited, traditional and conservative. You are currently showing qualities of shyness, modesty and reticence. When all of your fingers are spread out, you enjoy bucking convention. You have original flair and love to surprise – and sometimes to shock. You are currently revealing an uncompromising need for personal space and freedom.

Thumb

The thumb is the most important digit on your hand, and is the area that shows how much willpower and strength of character you possess. Do you wish to exert influence over your environment? Are you easily influenced by more dominating characters and discouraged by setbacks? How much are you the master of your own destiny? The size and shape of both of your thumbs will provide answers to these questions and much more. Remember to look at both hands to judge the thumb in personal (left hand) and professional (right) circumstances.

Large

A large thumb is one that is broad, solid and reaches at least halfway up the bottom section of the index finger. It is the single most important factor in your personal and professional success. A strong thumb can overcome any 'handicap' shown elsewhere in the hand.

Consider how many people go far in life by the force of their personality – this is the benefit of a large thumb. It provides you with the resolve required not only to survive but also to thrive. A large thumb provides mettle and backbone. With it, you will want to be in positions of authority and be recognized as someone important and effective. Your principal aim is to be seen as a strong personality – someone who is influential rather than easily influenced.

Small

A small thumb (one that appears short and slight in comparison to the rest of the fingers) is a sign of weak willpower and giving up too easily. If you have a small thumb, you should avoid looking for the easy way out. You must face up to problems, accept responsibility for your actions and work hard to build up self-confidence. You must have the courage to accept challenges and take part in life – to attempt things whether you succeed or fail. You need to resist the temptation to blame others for your current situation.

The tip

This section is considered large if it is longer than the lower section of the thumb. A large thumb tip reveals that you are strong, self-determining and wilful. You can achieve much through your forceful personality. You pride yourself on being a 'doer' but should be careful not to be too controlling or resort to bullying tactics, as you are used to getting your own way and having things done as you 'suggest'. Being subtle is not your greatest strength, so let those with patience and tact guide the more sensitive souls. When the tip is small, you have lots of ideas but have not yet developed the stamina, willpower or focus to implement them. You should avoid letting others have too great an influence over your life.

The clubbed thumb

There is another type of thumb tip – the clubbed thumb. This is a blunt, swollen-looking tip (often betrayed by an unusually short and wide thumb nail). With this hereditary feature, you tend to have extreme emotional reactions to life. At times, you feel alone because you sense that most others do not feel as intensely as you do, not do they wish to discuss the intensely emotional matters that swamp you. Others may brand you 'attention-seeking' and touchy, but you are a perfectionist who is easily frustrated when there is the slightest hitch in your plans. You may be terrified of not achieving your potential or of losing your composure.

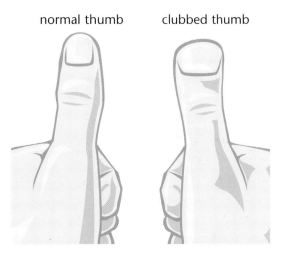

normal thumb   clubbed thumb

Avoid putting too much pressure on yourself and realize that trying to control your reactions (and booming temper) can lead to a situation that resembles an emotional pressure-cooker – a time-bomb just waiting to explode. You must avoid building up tension and instead find ways to relax.

The lower phalange

Whereas the tip of the thumb is associated with 'doing' and making things happen, the lower section is all about thinking and planning. To make a success of anything, there needs to be planning, and a long lower phalange gives you analytical ability and a logical mind (long fingers, page 110, and a long head line, page 42, will reinforce this). If noticeably longer than the thumb tip, you are a planner and strategist rather than a doer.

(long fingers, page 110, and a long head line, page 42, will reinforce this)

CURRENT POSITIONS

Thumb tip close to the palm
Self-contained; you are currently seeking solitude and privacy.

Thumb tip curled into the palm
Easily defeated; at present you would prefer to avoid responsibilities.

Thumb tip held away from the palm
Open and needy; you are currently self-confident and wish to encourage intimacy.

Index finger

The index, or Jupiter, finger has a great deal to say about your levels of assertiveness and ambition. It also is an indication of the extent of your pride, ego and self-esteem. Are you a leader or follower? How much do you believe in yourself? How far are you willing to go to get to the top? An average-sized index finger reaches halfway up the top section of the middle finger, and shows an ordinary level of self-confidence and pride.

Long

When long, you have a healthy ego but often want to dominate other people. The image you have of yourself is positive, be it your public image (right hand) or your inner sense of self (left hand). You are bossy and chase after positions of authority, full of conviction that you will succeed. You are a positive person who can motivate others with your enthusiasm and optimism, and you are in touch with your feminine side, although typically you exhibit 'masculine' traits.

You have a strong belief in providence, whether you follow a religion or your own faith. In relationships, it is important to be around people who respect your contribution.

Short

The impact of a short index finger depends upon the size of your thumb. If both are short, you are shy and have difficulty asserting yourself. If the thumb is long, you may go to extra efforts to prove yourself to the world. You are on a mission to be noticed, valued and given your due. Often this is bravado, a bluff, because deep down you may sometimes feel you are not good enough. Proving your worth to others is one way of bolstering your ego, but not the most productive in the long term. Your level of self-confidence and self-worth swings from one extreme to the other, but avoid being the hard-luck story that no one wants to listen to. In relationships, you should steer clear of those who want to dominate you and those who are all too easily dominated by you.

Often the index finger on one hand is short but long on the other, and this reveals a marked difference between the person you are in private (left hand) and the person you put on show to others (right hand). When the index finger is noticeably long or short, you are driven to succeed by a fear of failure.

Current positions

Index finger held away from the middle finger: Confident and independent; you are ready to take on the world and assert yourself.

Index finger tilted towards the middle finger: Shy and lacking in confidence and courage; at present you are seeking reassurance, feeling hesitant and unsure of your abilities.

Middle finger

Usually the longest finger on the hand, the middle finger reveals your attitude to your obligations and responsibilities. Can others depend on you? How seriously do you take your personal and professional commitments? An average-sized middle finger reveals that you are, in general, law-abiding and serious about the important things in life.

Long

A strong, straight middle finger reveals a strong morality and conscience, as well as an ability to be self-controlled and modest. You can usually be depended on to keep on the 'straight and narrow'. At work you aim to be conscientious, methodical and industrious, although at times you can doubt your abilities. In relationships, as in work, you pride yourself on being reliable, responsible and faithful. Others should recognize your ongoing need for periods of solitude, as you enjoy your own company. It is best that this finger is not too long, otherwise you can be a little morbid, and if signs on the head line corroborate (see page 49) you can be prone to depression.

Short

The middle finger is considered short when shorter or only slightly longer than both the ring and index fingers. You abhor rules and regulations, and at some point you may turn your back on what 'should' be done according to society's rules. You may not be the most committed of people when it comes to either working or romantic relationships. When the fate line is absent or only weakly marked (see pages 70 and 73), you have been keen to avoid a life path of routine or responsibilities, and some people may have 'dropped out'. For those with an earth hand (see page 19), the middle finger will sometimes look unnaturally short, but little should be read into this.

Current positions

Middle finger held close to the ring finger: Duty-bound and reluctant to let your hair down; sometimes an intellectual bore; you are currently feeling 'put upon', but secretly enjoy the feeling of being a martyr; you may be sacrificing your own needs and ambitions for the sake of another; learn to live for yourself and don't let others run your life.

Middle finger separated from the ring finger: Focused on personal projects and goals; you are now determined to enjoy life to the full and to put family duties and responsibilities to the back of your mind.

Ring finger

The ring finger holds court over all aspects of your creative nature as well as your desire to perform and command attention. Are you willing to be singled out to perform or speak in public? Do you have a personality that is attracted to the spotlight? Do you feel a need to take risks to grow as a creative person? Do you enjoy being centre stage? Examining the length of the ring finger will begin to provide the answers.

Long

Whereas those with a long index finger are driven to succeed by a need for power and control, if you have a long ring finger you prefer spotlights, fan mail and standing ovations for your creative endeavours. For you, the applause and recognition is greater than being seen as a leader. Many of you look for a creative outlet, especially if you work in an office environment. You want plaudits, not power, and you take risks because you know instinctively that you can grow as a person if you push yourself either artistically or creatively. You need to be noticed and adored and your vanity drives you to seek youth both in yourself and in your choice of partner.

You depend on the opinions of others perhaps a little too much, and in personal relationships the adulation and approval from another can sometimes be the thing you crave above anything else. Sports and musical pursuits may be of great interest, particularly those requiring good body-eye coordination. You may also have a strong interest in fashion.

Short

It is rare to find noticeably short ring fingers. One feature that is present is a fear of taking risks or putting yourself in view. You fear ridicule and criticism, so avoid public displays of affection and drama. You protect your private life and avoid prying people (particularly if your thumbs are held close to your palms – see page 113). Sometimes there is a strong need to get straight to the point and to avoid irrelevant nonsense at all costs (let those with long ring fingers appear to be insincere and obsessed with the trivial). You may adopt an intolerant view of art, considering most of it to be 'pretentious'.

Average

As always, there is middle ground, and an average-sized ring finger suggests that you need a healthy measure of attention and can put yourself 'on show' in the public eye if necessary; but you don't crave attention, like those with a long ring finger, nor are you hungry for control, like those with a dominant index finger.

Little finger

The little finger has domain over attitudes to (and around) sex, money, and business. Are you gifted in the art of persuasion? Do you have major sexual hang-ups from childhood? The little finger can reveal all.

Long

When long (reaching halfway up the nail section of the ring finger), you have the gift of the gab and can be expert in manipulating people and conversations. You may have an ability to write or speak in public (the head line will say far more about this), but two things are certain: you can talk and you know how to subtly persuade and influence others. You know that diplomacy is the art of letting someone have your own way! If your little finger is low-set it may appear misleadingly short, so take this into account.

Short

If the little finger is short and stubby-looking, you may not have the tact or the eloquence to win over others and may be shy in public situations, fearing that your intelligence may be judged. If it is short and delicate-looking, however, this indicates a late developer where emotions and sexuality are concerned. Your youthful enthusiasm wins admirers (as does your ability to converse with children), but your ingenuous or immature approach to relationships may not be so appealing to partners. At times, you want relationships to be 'perfect' and not have to deal with everyday problems. You need to address problems in an adult and realistic manner.

Low-set

Nowadays, a low-set little finger (when there is a noticeable step down from the base of the other fingers) is a common sight. This indicates that you are fixated on problems you had with one parent as a child. Sometimes a parent was physically absent, but more often they were emotionally remote. Many people feel the need to address this, but be careful not to let any parental 'issues' dominate your relationships.

Naturally twisted or crooked

This is a sign of being shrewd, calculating and sometimes a little devious. You can spot a bargain and negotiate a great deal, but you should avoid making money your first love.

Current positions

Little finger jutted out away from the palm: Independent and unwilling to be tied down; at present you are seeking space from an intimate, all-consuming relationship.

Little finger curled in on itself: At present you are not willing to let yourself get physically involved with someone. There is a fear of intimacy and sometimes a refusal to discuss current sexual problems.

Timing the Hand

The art of timing the hand is one of the most fascinating aspects of palmistry. It puts the all-important 'when' into the equation. Timing takes a great deal of testing and practice, but without it people would never get their questions answered. Remember that lines can change, so when you read a hand it will show personality and past and current circumstances as well as indicating future *possibilities*.

Timing methods

The most reliable lines on the hand to time are the life, head, fate and Apollo lines. If you are aged 30 or over, it is good to start with the first section of the fate line (below the head line), which covers the period from the late teens to the mid-30s. This time in life is often marked by important events that can be traced and verified using the fate line timing chart. The heart line is unreliable and difficult to predict. This may be because the emotional impact of relationships is often felt for many years after they have ended. It is hard to judge where one 'relationship' ends. The years in which gypsy lines (see pages 93–5) appear are a little easier to estimate because they fall under the little finger and are connected both to the mind (below the little finger) and the emotions (above the heart line).

Some points to remember

1 The main lines are divided into sections of seven years, with the age 35 considered a defining year in the hand.

2 Markings can change on hands. Difficult signs can disappear (as can positive ones), particularly when there is greater awareness of personality and needs.

3 First look to the character of the person to understand needs and responses.

4 Look to the psychology behind the event – the reaction not the event.

5 Look for back-up markings on other lines at the same dates. Synthesize these to gain a clearer overall picture of the events or themes at that point in life.

6 Check what happens next on the line, to judge how the event will possibly shape the future.

7 In all cases, note on which hand the marking appears.

8 In youth and old age, the appearance of the major lines will say more about current circumstances than studying the lines in fine detail.

Timing the life line

Possible events or periods shown on the life line

- Childhood difficulties

- Family events of great impact

- Academic achievements

- Realizing ambitions

- Leaving home

- Accidents

- Breaking away from restrictive situations

- Major relationship beginnings and endings

- Changing lifestyle or diet

- Buying property

- Business investments

- Retreating from or moving into the world

- Changing home or country

- Important journeys

- Periods of illness

- Health concerns

- Shocks

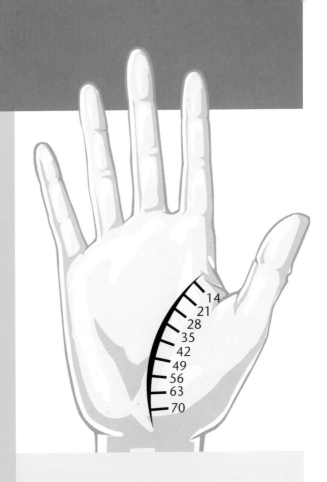

Points to remember

- The life line is timed from the top downwards.

- The lower section can be timed in conjunction with the rising fate line (using the latter's timing chart), and explores the time from the late teens to the late 30s.

Timing the head line

Possible events or periods shown on the head line

- Noted academic or professional achievements

- Changes of attitude or approach

- Starting over with a new outlook or religious conviction

- Times of greater professional or financial responsibility

- Recognition

- Financial gains and losses

- Injuries to the head or brain

- Suffering regularly from migraines or eye trouble

- Periods of stress, depression or breakdown

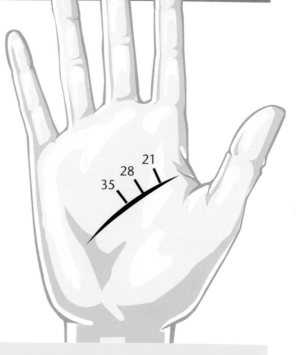

Points to remember

- The head line is timed from the thumb side of the hand across the palm.

- A short line will often only register events occurring until the early 40s.

- The most eventful years on the line are from 21 to 42.

Timing the fate and Apollo lines

Possible events or periods shown on the fate and Apollo lines

- Times of personal or professional responsibility

- Periods of hard work, productivity, less involvement and unemployment

- Interruptions to, as well as beginnings and endings of, important routines, jobs and relationships

- Times of personal, professional and financial independence

- Eventual outcomes of projects and partnerships

- Times of fame, fortune and recognition

- Periods of leadership or self-employment

- Changes in status and reputation

- Periods of creative fulfilment or general contentment (Apollo line)

- Financial gains and losses

- Important encounters

- Retirement: when, if and how it is spent

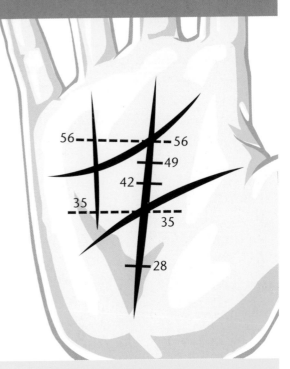

Points to remember

- The fate and Apollo lines are timed from the wrist upwards.

- The fate line may reach the head line at a later date than 35 if the head line is placed higher on the hand (usually as a result of it being separated from the life line at its commencement).

- The Apollo line is timed using the fate line's timing chart.

- With curved heart or head lines, the Apollo line may not reach these at the same age as the fate line, but it should be timed by connecting it to the fate line.

Further reading

Highly recommended guides to palm-reading

Clifford, Frank C. 2002: *Palmistry 4 Today*. London: Rider (also available from the website www.flareuk.com).

Fenton, Sasha, and Wright, Malcolm 1990: *Living Palmistry*. Wellingborough, UK: Aquarian Press.

Fitzherbert, Andrew 1989: *Hand Psychology*. New York: Avery.

Nishitani, Yasuto 1992: *Palmistry Revolution*. Tokyo: Tachibana Shuppan.

Reid, Lori 1996: *The Art of Hand Reading*. London: Dorling Kindersley.

Palmistry and work

Altman, Nathaniel, and Fitzherbert, Andrew 1989: *Your Career in Your Hands*. Wellingborough, UK: Aquarian Press.

Jaegers, Beverly 1996: *Beyond Palmistry II: Your Career is in Your Hands*. New York: Berkley.

Palmistry and health

Reid, Lori 2002: *Health in Your Hands*. Dublin: Newleaf.

Scheimann, Eugene, and Altman, Nathaniel 1989: *Medical Palmistry*. Wellingborough, UK: Aquarian Press.

Palmistry and children

Jaegers, Beverly 1997: *Beyond Palmistry III: The Hands of Children*. New York: Berkley.

Spier, Julius 1983: *The Hands of Children*. New Delhi: Sagar.

Other recommended authors

Books by Noel Jaquin, Julius Spier, Charlotte Wolff, Beryl Hutchinson, Mir Bashir, William G. Benham, Beverly Jaegers, Peter West and Fred Gettings will be excellent additions to your library. *The Encyclopedia of Palmistry* by Edward D. Campbell (New York: Perigee, 1996) is a thorough analysis of the work and findings of past and contemporary palmists.

Useful information

For details of the author's books, courses, seminars and talks in palmistry and astrology, visit www.flareuk.com, write to Frank Clifford at Flare Publications, 29 Dolben Street, London SE1 0UQ, UK, or e-mail him at info@flareuk.com.

Index

Acknowledgements

Hamlyn credits

Commissioning Editor David Alexander
Managing Editor Clare Churly
Editor Kate Tuckett
Executive Art Editor Karen Sawyer
Illustrator Fred Van Deelen
Designer Martin Lovelock
Production Controller Manjit Sihra

Author credits

Many thanks to the following who have made this book possible: David Alexander, my agents Doreen Montgomery and Caroline Montgomery, and all the staff at Hamlyn.

About the author

Frank Clifford is a writer, lecturer and Astro-Palmistry consultant. He began teaching himself astrology and palmistry at the age of 16 and wrote his first astrology book seven years later. Around this time he founded a publishing company (Flare) and edited/published seven books during 1999-2000, including the landmark *Astrology in the Year Zero* by Garry Phillipson, *The Draconic Chart* by Rev. Pamela Crane and two pop guides to the astrology of love and sex.

Frank's biographical data compendium is included in the world's best-selling astrology software Solar Fire, and his book *British Entertainers: The Astrological Profiles* (Flare, 3rd edition, 2003) is a popular reference work. Two further astrology titles, *The Midheaven* and *Birth Charts: Horoscopes of the Famous*, followed in 2004. His first full-length book on hand analysis, *Palmistry 4 Today* (Rider, 2002), was acclaimed for its original approach to the subject. It has been translated into Spanish, Dutch and Italian.

Frank has been interviewed on radio and TV discussing both astrology and palmistry, and been profiled in numerous magazines, including *The Guardian*. He writes the monthly horoscope column for the family magazine *Candis* and has written and recorded astrology columns and phonelines for *Marie Claire*. He co-runs The London School of Astrology and has devised a palmistry correspondence course. Frank is a regular at corporate events and parties reading palms and birth charts.

Frank can be contacted at info@flareuk.com or c/o Flare Publications, 29 Dolben Street, London SE1 0UQ, England. Details of his books, talks, workshops, parties and courses can be found at www.flareuk.com